W9-CHP-826

Sex on Fire

Finding Embodied Intimacy After Trauma

Leah RS Braun

Cover artwork by Brianna Darling
briannadarling.com

Cover design by Niki Lenhart
nikilen-designs.com

Published by Paper Angel Press
paperangelpress.com

ISBN 978-1-944412-83-8 (Trade Paperback)

10 9 8 7 6 5 4 3 2 1

FIRST EDITION

To learn more about the author and her work, visit
leahrsbraun.com

*This book is dedicated to every woman who doubts her power
and strength. May you claim it, may you speak it,
may you believe it.*

*And, to B and D.
Let this legacy forever be transmuted with your generation.
Have strong and compassionate voices and use them to protect
your children from things no child should have to endure. Raise
your kids to have voices and to speak up for those who don't.*

Table of Contents

Gratitude

T HANK YOU FIRST TO MY WOUNDERS, without whom I would not have a story, would not have found such an amazing healing path, and without whom I may not have gotten to know and love myself the way I have. That I can list you first is, I hope, a healing energy that you can use to resolve your *own* trauma, which must have been confusing and overwhelming for you, to have done the things you did in my life.

Thank you to my parents for stepping up and embracing your own accountability, for apologizing, and for continuing to champion me using my voice. Thank you for not being afraid of this book.

Thank you to my kids, who teach me so much every single day.

Thank you to my husband, Ciaran, whose amazingness is unwavering, even when the not-so-shiny stuff is showing for either of us. Though you came along later, you are my most valued teacher and I am honored every day to be your partner. I love you and I love that you create a safe place to use my voice, even if it is not always my prettiest one.

Thank you to my Tribe Members: Sarah O., Sacalame', Sonia. Your strength and cheering and mirroring and tea and chocolate and warmth made this process bearable and not so scary. Thanks especially to Priestess Sarah, who opened the floodgate for this project during Shadow Weekend.

Thank you to the Monday night dinner crew: Sarah F., Laura, Kari, Molly, Sarah B., and Kelsey. Love you guys and how we make dinner into teamwork and laughter each week. Xoxo.

Thank you to my sister for being outside of the whole thing, and therefore a good sounding board and a safe place to talk about family dynamics. I heart you so much.

Thank you to The Unruly Woman, who shepherded me toward publishing with her contacts at Paper Angel Press. And for all the synchronicity of our meeting! Crazy!

And, thank you finally to Laureen and Steven at Paper Angel Press. Laureen, you said the most phenomenal things about my manuscript, which made me, a first-time author, feel like a bright, floaty balloon for several days. Thanks to Paper Angel for being so willing to champion my story. Wow! All I want to do is write some more books, so there you go!

Your sex is on fire

Lay where you're laying
Don't make a sound
I know they're watching, watching

All the commotion
The kiddie like play
It has people talking, talking

You
Your sex is on fire

Dark of the alley
The breaking of day
Head while I'm driving, driving

Soft lips are open
Them knuckles are pale
Feels like you're dying

You
Your sex is on fire
Consumed
We're the ones, what's to transpire

Hot as a fever
Rattle of bones
I could just taste it,
Taste it

But it's not forever
But it's just tonight
Oh we're still the greatest,
The greatest,
The greatest
You,
Your sex is on fire

— Kings of Leon, *Sex on Fire*

Why tell this story?

T HIS IS A STORY ABOUT RAPE. We may as well dispense with any language that fluffs, minimizes, or attempts to soften the truth right from the get-go. I was raped repeatedly as a teenager and young adult, and 20 (or so) years later, I finally have the stones to talk about it outside the therapist's office. I am sad about that. Sad that it oftentimes takes 20 years of therapy to feel brave enough in our culture to tell the truth about rape out loud. It is our *rape culture* that requires the recipients of sexual trauma to keep quiet.

And, who the hell am I? I'm not a celebrity, I have a blog but nobody really reads it much, I am a regular white woman with a small business, 2 kids, a husband, and a Minnesota mid-century three-bedroom, one-bath rambler for a home. I am the height of ho-hum.

And yet, I am also amazing. My story matters. My healing is a testament. I know some things as a result of my rapes. I'm starting to grasp the reach of my power and truth sitting here typing these words.

Ultimately, this same amazingness is there for everyone to grab, regardless of color, sexual orientation, ethnicity, religion, country of origin, or wealth. The *amazingness* is equal, even if our degree of ease in today's society is *not* equal, depending on all those previously mentioned elements. When we all can know our *own* amazingness from within, our ability to express it shifts, despite our current society's imposed limitations. Let us all begin in the knowing, and to keep speaking it out. Let us keep listening to *all* those stories of amazingness. Let us listen first to the needs of the teller in getting her story out, and then let us help her do it, according to her needs.

Back to our rape culture. The cat-call on the street, the suggestive once-over leer, the offhanded sexual "compliment", the sex trafficking, the drugging of women in bars, the abusive relationships, the relationships with "prostitution contracts" — where it is understood that in exchange for financial security or an intact family one partner provides sexual access to the other, are all examples of violations that occur in rape culture. And, this behavior is somehow made okay by blaming the (female) victims or rationalizing the behavior as "harmless."

Our inability to look at this deep societal shadow serves to perpetuate the environment where sexual violation thrives. Even the Bible, in the story of Adam and Eve, implicates women (Eve) in general as being seductive, manipulative, wily, and persuasive —

getting men (Adam) to misbehave. The seeds of rape culture were sown a looooong way back.

So many women keep their rape and rape culture stories hidden because our society at large would rather just pretend that sexual harassment and assault do not occur. We blame the female victim for everything from the way she dresses to the way she holds her drink, it seems, in an effort to sink deeper into our denial about the frequency with which sexual violation happens. Which, according to the Washington Coalition of Sexual Assault Programs, it turns out, is about *once every two minutes in the United States.* So, there's a really good chance you know someone (maybe it's *you*) at the receiving end of sexual violence, violation, or harassment, and that that person has never told a soul.

Now too, we have so many instances of cyber-sexual violence and harassment that occur thousands of times each day with zero consequences for the abusers. And still, we have all collectively determined that this behavior is okay in our culture.

Beyond rape and rape culture, this is also a story about addiction, because that's what often happens after sexual trauma of *any* kind — either we victims go out and start using chemicals or behaviors like sex, cutting, food, gambling, or shopping to numb out and escape the pain of our experience, or we find *partners* who are addicted so we can focus on *them* and all their problems and how saintly and good we are for putting up with them. I ended up doing both of these things because I really, *really* loved the messy drama that gave me a cover story for my life.

Finally, this is a story about recovery and embodied sexuality. Because, as an author I really love (Glennon Doyle, Love Warrior) said recently in a radio interview, "My truth-telling is not in real time... you cannot share the most intimate details of your life that affect yourself and your family with the public until you have figured out the gift in it. As an artist, it is my job to serve people. I can't serve people with my truth until I have found the beauty in it." So I hope that my story is a gift and that at least one person out there in reader land might be helped, supported, and kept company in her own pain and healing by this narrative.

I tell this story to encourage other women (and men!) to use their voices. I tell this story to frame my own trauma work and continue to heal from the deep wounds of rape. I tell this story as an example for others that recovering from rape is possible with help and the right tools. I tell this story because a full life and a full, embodied, passionate sexuality are the right of every person and can be claimed as we all (men *and* women) heal our collective sexual shadow. I tell this story in order to share resources, support, strength, and encouragement on this journey.

Trigger warning

Many parts of this narrative could be triggering for other trauma recipients. Please proceed with caution and self-care. I believe there is value in moving through the story if it is relevant for the reader, but not at the expense of mental health. If you the reader want to proceed but are concerned about triggers, you might have a safe person "preview" the material first, or plan to move through the narrative with the assistance of a qualified mental health professional.

Let us begin.

Acknowledge the fear,
then speak anyway

THIS STORY IS HARD FOR ME TO TELL FOR SEVERAL REASONS, and here they are, in no particular order:

1. I worry about talking about myself too much — I'd much rather focus on someone else's stuff than my own.

2. I worry that sharing details about my story will hurt my family more than it hurts me to keep it quiet.

3. I am afraid that the details of my story may feel traumatizing for anyone reading it. I have watched this happen in a couple of therapy groups, even though I don't consider my account to be anywhere near as violent or traumatic as some others I've heard. I fear that I will be trolled, belittled, diminished, called crazy, a bitchy feminist, or told that

what happened to me did not actually happen — that I must be either lying or mistaken.

4. I'm scared that some people reading this will judge that my trauma is not really trauma because it is somehow not violent "enough," whatever that may mean.

So now with all that out of the way, there is no other reason to stall. I may as well get this over with so I can talk about the better stuff — the healing stuff — the (very hard, sometimes gut wrenching, not-for-the-faint-of-heart) way out.

My story begins when I was five.

Setting the stage for sexual trauma: Growing up in rape culture

MEMORIES FROM THE WAY BACK TIME are often hazy for anyone. There are a few that are like crystal for me, and this one was my first sexual encounter.

I had a sleepover with a friend one summer, and she and I slept in the same bed at my grandmother's big house. It was twilight, and we were chatting under the light summer covers.

"Do you want to play a game?" she said.

"What is it?" said I.

"It's the boyfriend-girlfriend game. We pretend to be boyfriend and girlfriend. I will be the boy."

She proceeded to climb on top of me and started kissing me like grownups do. I can't remember how long we kept "playing," but I knew it felt funny, like it should be a secret and we should not tell anyone. I also knew the game made my body feel really different — good. Squirmy. Funny *down there*. How else does a 5-year-old describe something like that?

I'm sure this little girl learned this game from someone else. Maybe she felt similar feelings of being "naughty" and wanted to share the behavior in order to perpetuate the good/different/squirmy feelings that might have been going on in her body too. My hope is that she learned the game from another kid her age and not at the hands of an adult or an older child who had a position of power over her.

At any rate, for better or worse, my body had an awakening that summer, and though it was no conscious fault or intention of this girl, she opened the door to my sexuality. At age 5. I've looked at this so many ways throughout my whole process. I've had numerous therapists and books reassure me that play of this nature between kids of the same age is natural and exploratory and harmless, however it always feels true that my troubles began here. That's an awfully young age to begin having sexual troubles.

It seemed like a switch was flipped inside my head and body, now that I could feel all these new sensations. I began to share the boyfriend/girlfriend game with other kids in my neighborhood. I wanted to play the game a lot, and I became good at ferreting out who was willing to play it with me. When I had these friends over or visited their homes, we continued role playing sexual/romantic scenarios based around shows we'd seen on television. We would even go so far as to put a big "Please Knock" sign on the outside of whatever door we were behind to give us some warning when adults were coming to check on us, which they rarely did.

This went on periodically with different girls until I was 12. It was something I looked forward to and often suggested with the friends who I knew were into it. Couple this activity with the fact that sex was on display in large and small ways in my house, and you can see that there was little sexual innocence for me to hold onto or protect. This background is important, because I believe it happens in a lot of houses, and it absolutely sets the stage (and some kind of strange permission) for the trauma that was to happen years later. Here are some of the things that happened in my home growing up:

- At holidays, I remember several instances of gift-giving involving sexy, adult lingerie, often given as a joke, most notably to my teenaged sister once or twice. So much so that when I was 11 and had saved enough money to buy my own Christmas presents for my family, the most special thing I could think of to give my sister was a lingerie nightie — see-through pink material with lace, a push-up bra, and matching tiny lace underwear. I wanted to give a grown-up gift to my grown-up sister, who I thought was the most beautiful person in the world. This was the example modeled for me, so that's what I chose. There is something messed up about that.

- My mom usually purchased a swimsuit calendar for her father at every birthday or Christmas to hang in his wood shop. (I later found out she had grown up quite aware that he was unfaithful in his marriage with several women — look how this culture permeates generations — it becomes insipidly *allowed*.)

- One Christmas, all the men in the family received subscriptions to Playboy magazine from the women in the family, complete with many winks, elbow nudges, guffaws, etc., while our whole family watched.

- I later went looking for those magazines in my parents' bedroom, and would read the letters and look at the pictures for hours when they weren't home. Once again, I was looking for that squirmy feeling, knowing that it was naughty and exciting, as well as something to keep a secret.

- My parents kept a copy of Everything You Always Wanted to Know About Sex But were Afraid to Ask on the family book shelf — I think I started paging through it around age 10. A tender age for a girl to be reading about prostitutes, johns, blowjobs, Men-wah balls, and fetishes. I'm all for being curious and informed about your own body and what it does as soon as that curiosity starts to happen. I just wish for me that all the other adult stuff would have been slightly less *available*.

I need to say something about my parents here. They were and are good parents. I was fed, clothed, loved, cared for, and cherished on the regular. My mom and dad told me often how much they loved me and how proud they were of me, and showed it in many ways. They shared their gifts with me. They showed up to school activities, took me places, and made sure I had a well-rounded life. I was given opportunities to do lots of cool things, and though money was often tight, I never felt like I missed out on anything. All of this sex stuff was so "normal" and so subtle, and it had so much to do with how my mom was raised as well as the marriage trauma of violence and visible adultery she witnessed... her normal surely colored my normal growing up.

My folks — especially my mom — and I have done a lot of intentional work around healing some of these wounds. Forgiveness — I of them, and them of themselves, abounds today. It took a lot of work to get to this place, though. More to come on that.

So, here are my bodily and sexual takeaways from childhood: Sexual behavior *feels* good, but it is to be kept a secret because it is bad. And, doing things that are naughty makes everything way more exciting, so it's a good idea to keep pushing the envelope, ever in search of *more*. *Also, women in general look best and most beautiful when they are wearing tiny swimsuits and lingerie, and they are valued and given attention from important men when they dress up this way.*

I hope for men that are reading this, you can clearly see the grooming that happens so early and with no one the wiser. And, for women who blame themselves for whatever sexual or gender trauma might have happened to you, in a culture like this, what chance do/did we have to recognize our own power and worth just for being human? I. can't. even.

One of the boys,
one of their toys

I THINK MY FATHER KIND OF WANTED A BOY. I mean, I have absolutely no doubt of his love for and pride in me. Since he wasn't into having tea parties and playing dolls with me, he showed me all the stuff *he* was into.

Don't get me wrong. I am forever grateful that he didn't use my gender as an excuse to not spend time with me or teach me what he knew. Because of my dad, I am an amazing skier, a fabulous dancer, a former basketball and volleyball player. I hunted and fished and swam and camped and hiked and skated my way through my youth with him, and those skills built a sense of confidence and comfort I have used in many rooms full of men and boys. Those skills were also the basis for a rewarding career in fitness during a time when there were not too many women hanging out in the weight room. My dad made me feel like I could do anything I wanted to do, and he was right! Thank God for this.

I guess my point is that there was also this weird sexual thing going on at the same time. I could be one of the boys, but I also liked and felt attracted to them at a very early age because of all that previous conditioning I talked about in the last chapter. So I felt this pressure to be both rough and tumble as well as sexy and alluring in order to fit in, and I got more attention for the latter than the former, it always seemed.

Whenever I played sports with men or boys, I always felt this undercurrent from them like they were thinking "Wow, she's cute *and* she can play basketball," instead of just being an equal on the court with them. I knew other girls who were respected for their basketball skills, but for me it felt like I was kind of a slutty basketball girl... I always got lots of "Hey baby", and "Nice work, honey" or even from one creepy basketball guy who held me in place by my waist under the net one time, "Grab the girls, right?" What most stands out to me of this experience is that I constantly needed to remind other players what my actual *name* was, and to please call me *Leah*.

My first real kiss with a boy occurred at the age of 9. He was 12. I went looking for it (those squirmy/naughty feelings). It was sweet, actually, we both hemmed and hawed around, hanging out on our bikes for some time before he and I both leaned in. Still way too early of an age, though, and further setting the stage for trauma later. However, I am relieved to declare that my first heterosexual kiss did not feel traumatic or seem to result in any adverse effects. Shortly after The Kiss, I moved to another neighborhood. Aside from meeting up one time at a playground where no other kissing occurred, we never reconnected.

I started going out on actual dates like a normal person around age 14, which again feels appropriate. Being the World's Biggest Nerd myself, I seemed to attract other equally awkward "nice boys" with braces and acne. Making out was the focus of most dates under the auspice of going to a school dance or movie. It seemed like a date was not a date without some kind of sexual expression, even though I had never gone beyond second base. This too strikes me as fairly "normal" for most teenagers, but that makes it all the more confusing about where the "normal" line stops and starts. How much is too much making out for a 14-year-old?

During the next several years, I could not seem to drop my affinity for flirtation and attention, so I am sorry to say that this behavior resulted several times in me hurting some of the persons I dated. I think there is a fair bit of this that just goes with being a teenager and figuring yourself out in the midst of raging hormones and playing at the complexities of interacting romantically with other kids, but it felt like a compulsion for me. I was also solidifying the belief that a feeling of sexual/flirtatious energy equated to a boy liking me and more importantly, *valuing* me. In fact, it was the opposite — several boys I dated would see me a couple of times, we would make out pretty heavily, and then they would move on. Because of my belief about physical exchanges equating with love and value, I felt a lot of pain a lot of the time when those boys stopped calling.

I really devalued *myself* a few times in the quest for the illusion of sexual/emotional value. I was the subject of a bet between two upperclassmen as a freshman in high school. We were all hanging out in the band room after school, and I was flirting with a tuba player named Don. He brought me back to a small practice room, and made me think I was hot shit for the better part of an hour, and then we ended up making out. I remember him saying that he couldn't ask me out on a real date because he was a junior and I was a freshman and he would lose all his cool points — or something like that. When we left the practice room, he bumped into his friend and he murmured "45 minutes" and I think they high-fived.

Another time, I was asked out by another upperclassman — a fellow drummer who I thought was cute and shy. After having a great time at a school dance together, he asked me to a winter formal. We went and had a good time then too (of course capping off the evening with heavy kissing and petting) Even after that though, he said we could date but we couldn't be "official" because I was a freshman.

Maybe this happened all the time with older guys being embarrassed to be seen with freshman girls. I don't know. I just know that the payoff of the sexual/flirtatious attention was for me enough to offset the *huge* devaluing of me by another. This should not have been okay with me, but it was, and that absolutely sucks. Nobody taught me how to discern that this kind of treatment was not okay.

Do you see where I'm going with this, everyone? Do you see now how the way gets paved for women to stay in abusive relationships? And, I had, by most standards, a pretty great childhood with no overt abuse or neglect at home. Can you imagine how little attention and charm it takes to hook a woman who has had a truly messed-up home life for all of her formative years? How good that initial attention and charm can seem and how scary it is for it to go away, even it is just crumbs? Even if it comes with actual assault? Anyway, it gets worse before it gets better, folks.

By this time, I was a freshman in high school. My two close girl friends and I were starting to grow apart because of lack of proximity and changing interests, and I was having trouble replacing those friendships. There was a pretty big gap in my life at this point in the area of acceptance and belonging. I felt like I fit in everywhere a *little* bit with all my activities (band, volleyball, basketball, skiing, and some loose social groups), but the sharing, attention, and *intimacy* of real friendship was suddenly gone. I was really lonely, and continued to hook up with guys whenever I could. I had a few "boyfriends" who lasted a month or two, and then would always find myself alone again.

To try to fill in the friendship gap, I seemed to be developing a knack for getting along well with adults. My parents' friends often enjoyed talking to me or listening to me play the piano. I nursed along a few crushes on some of my male teachers at school. I endeared myself to other school staff by getting good grades, raising my hand in class a lot, and generally being responsible with a sunny disposition. This worked well at church too, with youth group leaders and other friends of the family being happy to have me around. So, I managed to cobble together some sense of where I belonged, but still with an intense feeling of "in-between" — not cool enough to fit in completely at school, and not old enough to fully fit in with adults.

Let's move ahead to the summer between my freshman and sophomore year of high school. I am specifically going to share a ton of details about this most pivotal part of my story. I want to convey how strong these emotions were for a 15-year-old girl, and how we must all understand that teenagers are at an extreme disadvantage for making sound decisions about their actions while engaged in a hormonal and emotional firestorm like the one I am about to describe, coming from the rape culture "soup" in which I grew up. Note how smooth and manipulative all the steps were. I am also preparing myself for a flashback of these events, complete with all the intensity I felt when it was all happening. This is, to say the least, uncomfortable for me and not a place I enjoy going. I hope that it is relevant for many readers to give a glimpse into what this sort of traumatic memory feels like.

A whole new frontier

B RYAN SHOWED UP ON OUR PORCH on a rainy summer evening. He was a college friend of my father's and had ridden his motorcycle from his home in Atlanta to ours in Minnesota. He was reconnecting with my dad as well as visiting some old haunts in town, and was using our house as a base for his vacation. He was short, a bit stocky, dressed in a sleek black motorcycle rain suit, and carrying his helmet. I answered the front door when he rang the bell. My sister was home from veterinary school and we were the only ones in the house when he arrived. I can see very clearly in my mind's eye right now his face — his beard, his thick brown hair, and mostly, his piercing, direct eyes.

His demeanor was jolly and sarcastic — he had a quick wit and a direct manner and began talking to me right away like a fellow adult. His energy filled up the room for me. He and my sister and I proceeded to get acquainted while waiting for my folks to come home. All appeared normal, except I was tumbling into an *immediate* and very large crush on this guy.

As I begin to write about Bryan, I can see his face exactly as it was that night, and if I continue to "look" at him in my mind's eye, I begin to get a feeling of entrapment and powerlessness. His aura and energy, even through the lens of the past, feel oppressive and commanding, and it is hard to "look" away. It is hard still to not give him all of my power while I remember what happened.

The week proceeded with what appeared to be normalcy. Bryan spent time with our family in various ways as well as on his own doing whatever it was he had come up to do. Everyone had a great time with him and I was trying my hardest to win more of his attention. My mom even pulled me aside and asked if I had a crush on Bryan, that it was normal, but to keep my behavior in check. I denied it up and down and was completely mortified she had said *anything — ew, parents!* Still, inside, I was totally a-flutter just knowing he was in the same house.

A couple more days passed, and my parents were preparing to head out of town for one night with some friends who were having a party at a lake cabin a few hours away. This event had been planned for a while, but my mom had misgivings about whether she should go and leave me there in the house with Bryan. I was *praying* they would go while trying to remain cool on the outside. Apparently, my mom sat down with Bryan and shared her uncertainty, but he reassured her that all would be well and he could handle it just fine — *after all, it was just for one night.* Against her better judgement, my mom decided to go to the cabin with my dad.

I'm sure, dear reader, it is easy to see where our story is heading. I would like to point out here again there are so many steps that can lead up to trauma of the kind I'm starting to describe. The decision to leave me alone with Bryan has haunted my mother for years, and she has beaten herself up a lot for not trusting her gut that weekend and staying home. I have asked her why she felt she could not use her voice that day, and she doesn't know. The trajectory of my life would have changed a lot had they not left. Bryan was so smooth, she says, when they spoke, and so reassuring as well as being a bit smug, that she bought into his lie that I would be safe. I question here how her own history of trauma and growing up in rape culture allowed her to devalue her own truth based on the assurance of a smooth operator who was a trusted friend of my father's. I'm not sure how my father felt about the decision to leave me with Bryan — if he downplayed the risk of leaving his head-over-heels daughter alone with the very adult (23 years my senior) and inappropriate object of her affection, or if it just didn't even cross his mind that I might be vulnerable here.

Though I am not seeking to hurt my folks further with this narrative, this was abandonment on a profound level for me, which took me years to understand, heal from, and forgive. And, when this rift happened between my folks and I, it remained open and gaping — no one knew how to close it. Without the solid anchor of presence most kids find with their parents, I was left drifting on my own. This crippling loneliness sent me always toward the next abuser.

Remember that in cases like this, the child (yes, child, not Lolita, not slut, not seductress — the child) is never at fault. Teenagers do not have the developmental ability to sort through their emotions and make decisions to keep themselves safe in the face of such manipulation. If Bryan had just come up and touched my breast or

21

grabbed my crotch by way of greeting the first time we met, I would have been alarmed and categorized that interaction in the "bad touch" column, told my parents immediately, and he would have been out on his ear. Bryan had all the power of a completely developed adult brain when he saw how I acted around him based on my crush, allowed my advances and groomed me to keep the secret. There was no power exchange here because I had none to give to him in the first place.

Now, let's see where 15-year-old Leah is with our story.

I was so elated at the chance to be alone with Bryan I could barely sleep the night before the day we would spend together. My parents left in the morning, and the cloudy cool weather was ours for the having! I loved riding his motorcycle, and asked if we could take a drive up the North Shore of Lake Superior (how romantic!) and grab lunch. We talked and laughed the whole way, plus I got to hang onto him as tightly as I wanted from the back of the bike.

After the motorcycle ride, the afternoon was getting a bit too cold to be outside, so we rented a scary movie and got supplies to roast hot dogs and marshmallows in our living room fireplace. We continued chatting and laughing all through dinner, building proximity next to the fire (again with the romance!), and then later on the couch watching the movie, the horror genre giving me a perfect excuse to grab onto him at every startling surprise in the film.

After the movie, I remember laying my head on his lap as we continued to banter and giggle. Never once did he stop me or set a boundary. He just kept eating up my advances and allowing us to get closer and closer and closer. I was so captivated by the rush of my feelings, the attention from him, and my perception that he *valued* me like no one else ever had, that I never wanted the evening to end.

Time drifted, and it was getting late. I was both surprised and elated he was continuing to treat me like an equal, and decided I was absolutely in love with him at this point. We headed upstairs as if to call it a night, but I wanted to keep this going as long as I could. I asked if I could show him some of my music, and I brought my stereo in his room and sat on his bed while we talked at length about our favorite bands.

An hour or two later (by this time it was the wee hours of the morning, and I was more than a little punch-drunk from drowsiness and adrenaline), he said "Would you like to sleep in here tonight?" I pretty much thought my head was going to explode as I smiled at him and said "Yes."

I lay down next to him with my head on his chest, but I couldn't really fall asleep. I still could not believe this was actually happening. I lifted my head and looked up at his face. He looked at me and said "Would you like a real kiss?" The next thing I knew, his mouth was on mine, our tongues were mingling, and I felt like I was in some altered reality where dreams actually come true. We kissed awhile longer before finally breaking away and drifting off to sleep for an hour or two.

Whew. I have to take a deep breath or two after writing that. My body responds as if I were right there still. I chose to write that part of my story in such a romantic way because that is exactly how I felt when it was happening. That is why it is so easy to blame the girl when such cases of molestation are reported and charges are pressed. All the romance and physical arousal felt so good and I was sure it was what I wanted right then. I hope it is obvious how Bryan took advantage of his relationship with our family (access), a young girl's affection (a totally normal thing, by the way), and absconded with her (my, in this case) innocence. He had all the experience and power here. I had no chance, and had no idea what was to come later as a result (a hell of a lot of pain and suffering, that's for sure.) That night together may not have been a physical rape complete with intercourse or violence, but sometimes manipulation and molestation is worse for the victim. We spend years beating ourselves up, wondering how in the hell we ended up there and what we did wrong. Events like this are a total mind-fuck and can take decades to unravel. Now back to our story.

Bryan and I had to get up fairly quickly because my parents were coming home. We had a quick breakfast and tried to assume "normal" interaction. My mom and dad arrived back mid-morning, and we all went on about our day. Bryan was heading out the next day, so we were all about getting him packed and preparing to say good bye. I was also about to start volleyball camp that next week, so there was that also. Normal, right?

The next morning, Bryan saw me off (on my bicycle — there's an oddness to that I can never quite get around) to volleyball camp. In the garage, we had a minute alone. He thanked me for spending time with him, and kissed me once more, promising that if I wrote him letters, he would write me back and send me some mixed tapes (it was the 90's) with the bands we had talked about while sitting on his bed. I had every intention of holding him to it.

The Bryan Effect

L IFE GOES ON. Bryan went back to Atlanta, and my sophomore
year of high school started in the fall. True to my word, I wrote
to Bryan a couple times per week — spending hours pouring out my
teenage heart and soul to him on paper and decorating the
envelopes with intricate artwork. He wrote back about once per
month and started sending me music tapes.

During this time, I continued to date boys my own age and have
normal high school experiences mixed in with this other life no
one knew about. Bryan had a serious girlfriend that he went back
to in Atlanta as well as helping to care for his ailing mother. His
life continued normally as well, I believe.

A funny thing began to happen. Everything I did became something
to tell Bryan. I began to live my life through a kind of "Bryan"
filter. What would he think about the English paper I wrote? How
would he react if he were there to see the basketball game I played?

What would he want for Christmas? Would he like the sweater I bought? He likes neatness? My room became a shrine of order after having been a disaster area for years.

Bryan's letters were supportive and not overly long — he wrote bits and pieces about his family, his work, travels, and musical interests. He responded to my confused questions about our time together the previous summer kindly and with assurances that all was well, nothing to be concerned about, how much he liked me, and that he was willing to explore more if the time ever came. He cheered me up when I wrote about boys who had stopped calling, or someone I was interested in. He gave advice about letting go of boys who weren't interested and "looking out for number one."

Over the course of the next year and into the following summer, he visited twice: once for my sister's wedding, and again for his solo summer vacation. Both times, he kissed me again. Both times, the same excitement was there for me in the physical connection, the attraction and attention, and the secrecy. Still, no indication from him that any of this was wrong, and no boundary from him that we should stop. I was now 16. He was 39.

Summer Secrets

THE SUMMER BETWEEN MY JUNIOR AND SENIOR YEAR presented another series of yucky events. I got a job at the local minor league baseball field selling concessions at home games. It was a decent summer job and I got along okay with the rest of the staff who were also mostly young kids from mid-teens to early 20's.

Our boss was a guy named Daniel. Short, a bit stocky, sarcastic, funny, a direct gaze. Married. He reminded me a lot of Bryan, for whom I was always longing. For the first few weeks of the season, we were overstaffed and often times I got sent home because there wasn't much for me to do. It was toward the middle of the season when an important game with important people rolled around. I can't remember the exact circumstances, but I do remember that Daniel pulled me and one other girl aside and said we really had to "shine" at the concession stand that evening. Needless to say, I desperately wanted his approval and attention, so I did my absolute best.

I must have shined well enough, because here is the thing. There was intrigue, flirtation, secrecy, and some making out that started happening with Daniel and I very soon after that game. That part is all pretty hazy to me today. What ultimately happened and remains crystal clear to me was that shortly after those few "makeouts", I found myself exchanging oral sex with him in the dingy back office of his restaurant on the other side of town.

I had only ever tried oral sex once before with a previous boyfriend. We were both exploring (one of the few times I felt like a somewhat normal sexual teenager) and everything felt okay. Boundaries were respected, and we both got a little nervous and did not progress beyond that point. Also, people knew we were dating, my parents liked him, and he treated me well even though we did not last more than a few months.

With Daniel, the whole experience was gross. He was behaving as though he was giving me some great treat when in reality I did not feel good, was afraid someone was going to walk in on us, and the physical sensations were pretty awful, to say the least. After he was done with me (I had made him believe I climaxed so that he would stop), I ended up letting him come in my mouth just to get the whole thing over with. It never occurred to me I could say "no" and leave, because I thought I had *wanted* this to happen. I felt like I had to follow through or he would think less of me.

I was 17 years old, having oral sex in a dirty office wondering how I ended up in this place, and still concerned about what Daniel thought of me. That is rape culture.

I was ashamed, disillusioned, and humiliated, and so sad that the experience with Daniel wasn't at all the same as what had happened with Bryan. I couldn't re-create the connection. It wouldn't be the last time I would try, either, with several others. Remember, I was indoctrinated from as early as age five to believe that the most valuable form of attention or connection I could receive from a man was sexual attention. That type of brainwashing does not go away easily. I wish so hard that I could have seen this series of events at the time for what it was: Rape. Pure and Simple.

After the rape happened, I pushed it aside and tried to simply move on. I told no one, though I think some of the other managers at the ballfield had a clue as to what had been going on. I shoved down all of the disgust, self-loathing, and sadness, and just pretended the whole thing never happened. I made it to the end of the summer without much further interaction with him, and that was that. I was 17 years old.

Pushing the Envelope

I WAS JUST GETTING BACK INTO MY SENIOR YEAR OF HIGH SCHOOL when it was time for Bryan's annual sojourn up north. The school year had begun just fine, all things considered, but I could barely contain my excitement about Bryan's visit. I had gotten my braces off, changed my hair, and generally was hoping I looked a little more grown up… again, for *him*.

The week began as his visits usually did — all family members getting reacquainted with him and generally doing fun things together in various combinations of personnel. There was one night I needed to go to the mall for something, and Bryan offered me a lift. We hung out for awhile, walking around, browsing the stores and chatting it up. When we were back in the car driving home, I asked him to pull over before we got to the house.

I had been holding in my secret about Daniel for a long time, and I really wanted to tell *someone* so I didn't have to sit alone with it anymore. I knew Bryan was probably a "safe" choice because he did not know Daniel and there was no way he was going to expose me. I spilled about the whole thing, and when Bryan asked me why it had happened I said "because, Bryan, he reminded me of you."

I think I remember a movie soundtrack swelling up in the background, because Bryan swept me into his arms and began kissing me like he was never letting go. When we came up for air, Bryan said he would be happy to take me somewhere and do whatever it was I wanted him to do with me, and how sorry he was about Daniel. He has always maintained that he made that offer because he was protecting me from finding some other random guy and acting out in similar fashion. Bryan was willing to "jump on the grenade," so to speak, for my own safety and well-being, and be the adult with whom I explored this rampant desire. How noble.

Well. That was some new information. I had to think about it for about a nanosecond before I said "yes" and we started making a plan for getting a few hours alone together. We got back to the house, tried to calm down, and headed inside as if nothing had happened. We decided to take a day trip on the weekend up the North Shore again, find a hotel, and have sex. This gave me a couple of days to further build up the intrigue and the romance in my head to epic proportions. When Saturday finally came, I was figuratively jumping out of my skin.

I think my parents might have been asleep during this period of several years. I'm not sure if I was just really good at appearing normal, or if I was giving off signs that all was not well and they had their own stuff going on and did not notice. Because I was so wrapped up in Bryan and now this recent summer episode with

Daniel, I don't remember much of what was going on in their working or social worlds, other than money seemed to always be tight and finances were a pretty constant source of stress, even though we lived in a very nice home, had food on the table, and did fun things fairly frequently. Maybe it was that stress that allowed them to look the other way at the time Bryan and I spent alone together. Maybe my mom was able to push down her doubt because she didn't want to think about the possibility that her original misgivings about Bryan were correct and he was co-opting her youngest daughter's affection and loyalty right under her nose.

It is also relevant to note that during this time I had a steady boyfriend, who was also my first sexual intercourse partner. I am forever grateful for this individual, because he gave me the gift of a "first time" I can look back on with absolutely no shame. We were nearly the same age, I believe he truly loved me, and I cared for him a great deal. The moment was special and we were both responsible about birth control. I was a bit more experienced than him, admittedly, but we were both exploring honestly and figuring out our bodies. The only part I regret is being raped by Bryan while still going out with him. I now realize that while I knew what was happening with Bryan was wrong, I was completely powerless to define it or stop it, so deep was the trust, admiration, and worship I had placed upon him. The words "Total Mind Fuck" are the only three I can find to describe what happened next.

Saturday morning arrived and Bryan and I were out the door, this time in his car and not on the motorcycle. The leaves were beginning to turn and it was a crisp, sunny fall day. We rode about ninety minutes north of town, and stopped to look at a popular lighthouse along the way. There was much hand holding and kissing and canoodling. Then, while we were walking around,

Bryan made the offer that if this did not feel right, we could forget it. Maybe this took some pressure off him in his own mind. Maybe he was having some doubts of his own. I don't know, but at this point, I was his hook, line, and sinker, and I think he knew it. I said I appreciated the consideration, but I loved him and I wanted to move forward and find our hotel — I was ready to complete my fantasy, or so I thought.

We found a small place a few miles up the road from the lighthouse. They had a vacancy sign, so we checked in. I was so nervous I wanted to throw up. We got to the room — the hot tub suite, no less, and he started undressing me right away. "You're beautiful", he said, as he slid me out of my underwear and took off his own clothes, revealing a regular middle-aged body — a far cry from Adonis, but he was so smooth with all his words and experience, I didn't really think to care about that.

I have to pause a moment, because I can feel this in my body as I write it. My stomach is in knots, I know what part is coming and it's not good, and I know it is a long time before this story finally ends. I know the power over me Bryan has at this point in the narrative, and I fear it is looking like I wanted this all along. I thought I did. I wanted the fantasy... the story of it all... the daydream, just like many teenage girls do. I wanted the romance and the attention and the value and the compliments and the fancy-ness this man was offering to me. He might as well have been mainlining heroin into my veins at that moment, so great was my need for everything he was dishing out except sex. Such a slick pusher was he. He was about to push me right over the edge.

So, after all this build-up, I felt like a deer in the headlights just before the actual sex. Everything got very real, very fast. I had been having sex for a few months with my high school boyfriend, so I knew some of the things to expect, but what surprised me was how *un-good* the actual sex felt with Bryan. The only word I can use to accurately describe it is "icky." Kind of painful at moments. Again, I didn't get much enjoyment out of it, even though he tried hard. I felt defective, somehow, that I could not deliver on the ecstasy I thought he expected. I was glad when it was over and we could get back to the kissing and snuggling and laughing part of things, which was what I really wanted. We spent a couple of hours hanging out in the room, and then got dressed and left when it was time to go.

The odd thing was, I compartmentalized the actual sex right away. I pretended it didn't really happen, because it didn't live up to the fantasy, and I felt I was to blame for that — like there was something wrong with me that I did not respond like I was "supposed" to. I just wanted to go back to enjoying and fantasizing about all the "other" romantic stuff. Bryan seemed pretty happy and things remained close between us for the remainder of his visit. I'm still a little baffled that either we were able to put on a good show of normalcy after we got back from that afternoon, or that my parents were so invested in looking the other way. Nobody's feathers were visibly ruffled. I don't know what my mom or dad were feeling, if anything, at this point.

A couple of days later, Bryan left for his home in Atlanta and everyone returned to their "normal" life — him still involved with the same serious girlfriend and me going back to being a high school student with a boyfriend of my own. The dishonesty of dating that boy and being in love with Bryan were beginning to wear on me, and also Bryan and I were ramping up the content of our letters. The content of communication now included sexual fantasy as well as regular daily fare. The frequency of our letters increased as well. I broke up with my boyfriend a couple of months after Bryan had left from his visit. He continued to be involved with his girlfriend in Atlanta. This was beginning to wear on me too.

Bryan and I also began talking on the phone when my parents were not home. So much so that he sent me a calling card (again, the 90's, before cell phones were the norm) so I could reverse the phone charges and no one would be the wiser. We spent hours talking, laughing, flirting, and fantasizing with each other. Things intensified so much that we began to try to figure out how I could come down to see him and where he lived in Atlanta.

Years after all of this occurred, I found out some things about child molesters. They have patterns. They look for access to kids, like being a coach, a teacher, a priest, a child-care worker, etc. They are charismatic, fun, and very confident. They endear themselves to parents and other family members and create a sense of trust. They groom the kids they molest by luring them in with a treat of some kind. For little kids, that might be candy or toys. For me it was attention and compliments and adult conversation. Then, they set up little secrets. For example: "I know you're not really supposed to to have/do this (candy, toy, car ride), but it'll be okay this once, and it's just between us." When I told Bryan about my boss Daniel, he had his secret and he knew I would never willingly tell my parents about us. I trusted Bryan completely and he didn't even have to try. I was the proverbial fish in the barrel for him. I don't believe he targeted other kids — his lifestyle didn't include a lot of access to children and teens. He was an opportunist, and I was his opportunity. He may have had actual feelings for me at that time, but all of the feelings resulted in the rape of my mind and my body. He took everything he wanted to have. Any healthy adult would have seen my advances early on, shared concern about it with my parents, and taken action to make sure nothing ever came of my crush. Instead, I was led down a road to almost complete personal annihilation as a result of being a human, female, sexually blossoming teen in a culture where molestation and rape were (and are still) dirty secrets that no one wanted to believe.

By this time, my spring break was coming up, and I asked my parents if I could spend it with Bryan in Atlanta. He lived in his parents' home where he and his brother were caring for their mother who was in the later stages of Alzheimer's disease. There was a female live-in nurse present as well to assist with that care. I made up some excuse about looking at a couple of colleges or something equally as lame, as well as voicing the fact that there were plenty of people in the house. They said yes, and *actually let me buy a plane ticket* with the money I had saved up from babysitting and my summer job. The irony today is that I spent my own money to spend time with this predator. I managed to personally finance the continuation of my own rape. How fucked up is that?

With the plane ticket purchased and the scheduled trip just a few weeks away, my mom was beginning to listen to her inner voice again. Thank God no one was there to talk her out of it this time. She went into my room to look for some of my letters from Bryan. I think I must have wanted her or my dad to find them, because I never made any effort to lock them away. I kept several recent letters on a shelf near my bed so I could read them often.

They read the letters while I was at school. To this day, I'm not sure exactly how I survived the next part of the story.

A fantasy obliterated

T HE SCHOOL OFFICE SENT A MESSAGE to one of my teachers that my parents were coming to pick me up, and to grab my stuff and be waiting for them. I felt an immediate sense of doom. I was not wrong to feel that emotion. My parents came, and not a word was said on the drive home.

I need to pause and breathe here. What happened next felt worse than both parents dying, I think, and I continue to feel the dread in my stomach as I prepare to relive, in writing, the terrible events of that afternoon. There have certainly been plenty of stories that were physically more horrific than the piece I am about to tell, but it sure did not feel that way on this particular day. My life was about to end as I knew it.

When we got to the house, all three of us went to the living room and sat on the couch. My parents together on one end (it was a sectional, this is an important image to visualize), and me facing them all the way down on the other end. My mother pulled out a letter, and asked me to explain myself.

I can still see clearly the absolute agony in her face and the tears in my dad's eyes. There is no feeling like the one I felt that day. I knew my guts were about to be emotionally ripped out.

I spilled the whole story, from the very beginning of that first trip he took to our house and the night they left us alone. I talked about how we were in love and had been talking on the phone, and I choked out the truth that Bryan and I had sex during his most recent stay with our family. I watched my parents' faces crumble with that last admission. I knew that nothing would *ever* be the same. I felt so ashamed and knew that all of it was my fault.

Look at this young girl cowering on the couch, crushing herself down as low as she could into the corner as she poured her heart out and tried to protect all the adults. None of this was her fault. She was simply a teenager up to her neck in rape culture. This is how it happens. She — I — would spend the next 10-plus years in a destructive spiral, beating herself up over and over with the shame she felt and trying somehow to continue to get the highest form of love and adoration she was taught existed — through sex. Can we all please take a moment to put our arms around this lovely and precious girl? She is one example of many such girls who become lost in ways too similar to this, and this account is mild by most standards. What does it take to stop this insanity and show every girl her true worth? No one should have to give sex to get value. No one.

I think they said things about the lying I had done, and asked me "why?" I told them I just didn't want anyone to get hurt, that Bryan was one of my dad's closest friends, and that I knew they would be mad if they found out and then Dad would lose his friend. I also remember saying "This is really hard. I'm only 17."

Here's what happened next:

1. I was told that I would be driving myself straight to the clinic for an emergency STD test.

2. I went alone and tried not to lose it when the very nice nurse practitioner asked a few routine questions and drew blood.

3. I went from the clinic straight back to school to take an anatomy exam that was scheduled for that day and was a large part of my grade.

4. I set the curve on the exam with the highest score in the class. Compartmentalization was a coping skill I had honed to a fine art, apparently.

The following weeks were spent in a foggy sea of numbness and grief. I lost my parents, effectively, and I lost Bryan, at least for the immediate future. My parents were leaning on their friends for support, comfort, and emotional processing. Bryan was not allowed to speak to me. I was upon my own island with no row boat in sight. I never thought about killing myself, but I couldn't see how I was going to survive either. I floated through school and tried to mentally escape as much as I could. At home there was just pain and more pain.

The only glimmer of light during this time came from my band teacher, Mr. Leibfried. He was my favorite teacher in the best way — I knew he cared about *all* of his students and I had been in his class since 7th grade. He must have sensed something was very wrong because he pulled me aside one day and said "Leah, you look a little down in the mouth lately, is everything okay?"

"No," I said. "But I can't really talk about it."

"Well, I hope things get better soon," he responded. I'm pretty sure this little exchange was the only thing that helped me to see there was more in my world than grief and loss. Just the fact that he noticed and cared and I didn't have to *do* anything for that attention helped so much. We need more men in the world like Mr. Leibfried.

So all this while, Bryan was just hanging out in Atlanta. I have no idea what he was thinking — if he was worried about me, about him, or just enjoying his life. My dad, at one point, mentioned it was a good thing he lived so far away because if he had lived nearby he would have been dead. My father owned a couple of guns. I'm glad it did not come to that, but now that I am a parent myself, I can totally understand the motivation for murder in a situation like this. I wish today that both of my parents would have been more awake and trusting of their own intuition before the rape happened.

Meanwhile, I was still completely in love with Bryan. That never went away. I missed him with an ache that is hard to describe — probably because I was floating in a sea of grief on my own. I missed terribly the secret world of fantasy we had created where I got to feel mature, sexy, desirable, and worldly. I just wanted to go back to having that secret between the two of us.

My parents knew this, and they were afraid that I would find a way to run to him. The thought of running away had never occurred to me, actually. I still saw my parents as having most of the control over my practical life — and I was responsible enough then to understand the logistics of running and how I just didn't have the resources to make it happen. I also thought Bryan would disappear anyway because this was all so hard and I had somehow screwed everything up.

What happened next is that after a time, my parents allowed Bryan and I to speak again. Everyone spoke on the phone. My parents to Bryan — I was not party to that conversation that I can remember. And then, Bryan and I. The details of what Bryan and I talked about are gone. I was so in survival mode that everything for the next few months is just a blur. What I do remember is that somehow, Bryan and I were allowed to meet again that summer. (It just keeps getting weirder, I know.) Again, my parents were living under the fear that if they restricted my access to Bryan completely, I would run to him and they would lose me forever. So, Bryan made plans to drive up that July, pick me up, and take me to St. Paul for a few days alone.

When I think today about how that trip went down, I just want to vomit. I still cannot wrap my head around the oddity of my parents knowingly giving me away, in effect, to this sick and twisted human. Their fear of losing me must have been greater than their protective instincts. I was also 18 by then and legally an adult, so I don't know if that factored into their decision as well at that point or not.

Bryan arrived this time on a sunny July morning. I was happy to see him, and hopeful that everyone would just get used to the idea that we were going to be together and that was that. There are moments in life when I think we all step outside of ourselves and just stare at whatever's happening and think "What the hell is going *on?*" This pivotal moment for me was sitting on the couch with

Bryan and my parents, having tea, while they were prepping to see their 18-year-old daughter off for four days alone with the man who legally raped her. I don't know what kind of numbing out/compartmentalizing/denial kind of energy that took on their part, but I bet it was a lot. I don't know how my dad stayed in his chair. I don't know how my mom drank her coffee. I just wanted to hit the road. So, we did.

We drove to St. Paul and set up camp at one of the downtown hotels. Once we got out from under my parent's' gaze, I was free to sink into the romance fantasy again. We did touristy kinds of things — the zoo, the river, dinner out. And, there was, of course, more sex.

I only remember bits and pieces of the trip. The clearer images include more and varied sexual acts — him introducing me to things I had not yet tried with anyone else and that the physical intensity was beginning to be a thing — that I wanted more of that along with all the continued attention and romance. The other piece that stands out was him sitting me down at the zoo and telling me he was leaving a day earlier than planned. He made the excuse of needing to get back to family and work, but I really think everything was getting a bit too real for him as well and he was finally getting less comfortable (and perhaps a bit ashamed?) of the situation he was in with me. I could tell he was pulling away somewhat. He drove me back home and lit out immediately for Atlanta.

And so it was. While I felt sad to see him leave, on some level everything was more comfortable with him gone. I continued to write to him often, and he wrote me back a few times. I was so busy with my summer job and preparing for college in the fall that

I didn't have a ton of time to obsess about him. Thank God for small miracles. This was not the end of our story, and the worst was yet to come, but I did at least take a small intermission.

College in the trauma soup

O FF I WENT TO EXOTIC IOWA. I was so relieved to get out of my home town and be on my own. The school I chose was small, picturesque, and expensive. My grades and activities got me a decent financial aid package for the first year, and I think all members of our household needed a break from each other, so it was a good idea to move away for a while and to still be in the somewhat controlled environment of college.

I did the normal college things — I met all kinds of people, took classes, practiced being a beginning adult. I loved my studies and found a loose circle of friends, though I still found it very hard to be close with women. I couldn't understand why that was. I had one close friend and a bunch of acquaintances. I played in the jazz band and played pick-up volleyball on Sunday nights. I was still kind of lonely, so I filled that space the way I learned so well — with men and sex.

It seemed that the only men I found or who found me were committed to someone back at home. I was a welcome distraction and a space-filler for them, but no more. I am so sad, still, that this was okay with me. That the attention and the sex were enough to offset the fact that I was never anyone's priority. I was never my *own* priority.

I was so afraid of losing the "fix" of the attention by setting a boundary and saying *no* that I just made it all okay. I was cool. I wasn't outwardly jealous. I was available. I said yes a lot. I never knew how to just date someone. I never knew how to build an actual intimate relationship built on respect and honesty. That's not to say I didn't experience love or caring in my way — I fell hard for one of these men and he seemed truly torn about whether to choose me or his at-home girlfriend. I wish today that I would have chosen for *myself* and said "No thanks. Call me when you are a free agent."

I think that's the root. I kept waiting for others to choose me because I never learned how to choose myself. It was such a strange contradiction — the confident, poised, intelligent young woman who could hold her own in any room full of guys was pretty much a doormat when anyone offered up the slightest compliment or gave me the head-to-toe suggestive eyeball. That was the attention I had learned was best, so that's what I sought out. I was always surprised when that kind of attention turned out to be the worst in the end. The result of that kind of attraction was universally damaging. By the time I figured that out I was in so deep I could not escape or change on my own.

Bryan was still lightly in the picture during freshman year. I wrote him a few letters, and he came up for a very short visit. It was okay, but over in a day or two, and then we drifted apart for a time. Instead, I found other older men to fill the gap he left. I became an expert in what is called "running energy." It is a way of talking to someone to find out what their receptiveness is to flirting and building attraction. Healthy people with strong boundaries are not generally susceptible to this sort of thing, so one can imagine the type of men I was finding.

I had a biology professor who was willing to get close to me, though he stopped short of having sex with me. There was a guy at my summer job between freshman and sophomore years in college who was playing me and another woman on staff at the same time. Real winners, all of them.

Then, there was Jack.

Somebody please take care of me

J ACK WAS A LONG-TIME FRIEND OF MY MOM'S. They had grown up together working summers at a resort in northern Minnesota, and he often was hanging around the fringes of our family for things like birthdays, some holidays, graduations, and the like. Since he lived in-state, his visits were short. He also had a cabin on the same lake as my grandparents and it was a small, close-knit community up there. We often saw him at town functions when we visited my grandparents.

Backtracking a bit in the timeline, my parents sent me to Jack's house for a summer weekend when I was 17 to spend a few days learning how to mountain bike. Fun trip, generally harmless (although, *what the hell?* with all the access to single adult men — even though nothing happened that trip, that was an incredibly risky thing for my folks to approve, regardless of how much they trusted this man or thought they knew him). We biked, we ate, we watched movies, we went to sleep. However. I could feel the hint of the same kind of energy I felt around Bryan. Even though nothing blew up that weekend, the foundation was being laid for more trauma.

Moving forward again to the summer after freshman year of college, Jack offered to have me come up again for a biking weekend. I was 19, and our family was still trying to heal from the events around Bryan. My mom actually took the time to ask me where my head was about such a weekend, but I assured her nothing funny was going on. (*And, how tragic that now by default everyone felt like they had to check with Leah to see if she was going to seduce another friend of the family. Just so much brokenness to witness there.*)

Internally, I'm not sure what I thought would happen during my stay with Jack. I did not set out to be sexual with him the morning I left for his house. I headed up north and looked forward to being on a bike out in nature.

I met Jack in a town not far from his out-in-the-sticks-on-a-lake house. We got all my stuff back to his place and picked up a spare bike on the way from a friend of his. We enjoyed a warm-up ride near Jack's house to prepare for the big ride the following day.

At one point in the ride, I stopped my bike and was quite taken with the beauty surrounding us — bright, warm sunshine, tall leafy birch trees casting floaty shadows all over a quiet dirt road. I turned to look at Jack and said "Do you ever marvel at all this beauty?" He looked at me in a funny way, and said "Yeah, I do." That is the moment when everything began to shift.

Here's what is so hard about my time with Jack. It felt completely nurturing. Soft, wonderful, caring, and warm. Make no mistake that this "relationship" was just as inappropriate, if not criminal, as what had transpired between Bryan and me. The age difference was ridiculous — 33 years this time, and I later found out he had dated my mom when they were growing up and that they had a physical relationship. This fact created a mountain of shame for me the size of Mt. Everest. I still cringe in disgust when I think about that particular truth. Even though the sexual part with me and Jack (which we will get to) was never violent and at the time felt consensual for me, again we have a man with loads of adult experience at age 52 sexually involved with a 19-year-old. And, he withheld details about his involvement with my mom before she was married. I have had to process through a lot of anger at my mom for keeping an ex-boyfriend close to our family and adding to the trauma soup. My feelings toward Jack are a still a very confused mixture of deep anger and betrayal combined with deep gratitude for the nurturing he dished out so readily when I really did need it. (Maybe that is how drug addicts feel about their pushers?) It is so hard to have both sets of emotions exist at the same time. It is a big "yuck" factor with which I still struggle. I wanted so badly to have the fantasy of playing house and having a man care about and for me, and being sexual with older men allowed me to live inside the fantasy for a time. Also, the current theme throughout continued to be "I can have all the nurturing, care, and attention I want as long as I pay for it with sex." This was becoming hardwired into my brain. Clinically, this is known as Trauma Bonding and Trauma Repetition — two common symptoms of Post-Traumatic Stress Disorder.

So, by this time after Bryan and a year of other men in college, I was highly adept at reading sexual energy. I could tell after the moment on the dirt road that Jack would be open to maybe acting on it. I think that is where my trauma "switch" flipped on. I still wasn't sure what would happen, but I was waiting — anticipating.

Later that evening, we ate dinner and continued to talk, laugh, hang out. Jack had an amazing sauna just down the path to the lake from his house, and we had planned to use it. This had happened during the first bike-riding weekend a couple of years back, but this time there was a new expectancy in the air.

Jack fired up the sauna and we spent an hour or so going in to sweat it up and out to cool off. I felt so fresh and cleansed. I was thoroughly enjoying the night air in the screen porch. We weren't too chatty — just soaking up the sensations and the cricket sounds and the breeze.

I began to rubbing some lotion on my legs and I could feel him watching me in the semi-dark. Next thing I knew, we were spooning and snuggling on the bench in the porch. It was all unfolding slowly, deliciously.

Let's pause again. I remind the reader that I am writing this narrative the way it felt to 19-year-old me. It reads like a romance novel at times, doesn't it? You might even find your body responding to the words and the descriptions in some way — that's natural for all of us when we think of romantic and/or arousing images. I also remind you that all this romance was covering and clouding a horrible, wounded, rapey reality.

The reality was that I had never healed the wounds that Daniel and Bryan left, that I desperately needed intervention from healthy, qualified adults, and that my emotional/spiritual maturity in many ways was now stuck at the age of 15. I looked and acted outwardly like a young adult, but I had no idea what was really going on inside me or the profound and far-reaching damage that had been done to me.

Even if I had had some inkling of the blackness spreading inside, I had no idea where or how to ask for the help I truly needed. Instead, I went to the places that looked the best and easiest and most readily available. I just wanted to feel better — to feel good.

My parents (inadvertently, I believe) had made sure that this twisted kind of "help" was always within arm's reach whenever I needed it by who they allowed into our family. I never did become a drug addict. I didn't need to — sex, love, and romance were quickly becoming my drugs of choice. It was just easier to surrender to the high of a new fantasy than be alone with all the pain.

After another hour or so on the bench, we went back up to the cabin, and I slept in his bed that night. No sex. Not yet. But paving the way quickly, for sure.

The next morning, we got up and prepared for the big bike ride. Jack made me the most delicious pancakes I had ever tasted and got all our gear ready to go. We drove for about thirty minutes to get to the bike trail — my head resting on his lap the whole way, and him tenderly stroking my hair. We spent the day on the trail, stopping here and there for food and refreshments. We were both feeling pleasantly wiped out and in a hazy affection/attraction fog at the end of the day. We drove back to his place and cleaned up for dinner.

The evening passed with a blissfully relaxing dinner and conversation. I think we watched a movie. When it was time for bed, he led me again into his room and said "No clothes tonight." I think I just nodded my head and let him undress me.

We kissed, touched, and eventually had oral sex. That part was fine — nothing really out of the ordinary, for me anyway. It was over after a while and we drifted to sleep. (What was *ordinary*, at this point? Any kind of reference for *ordinary* had slipped away years ago). I wanted to remain in the cocoon of Jack's bed and home and nature sanctuary forever — so pleasant was this weekend oasis. And yet. I knew the storm was coming and my stomach began to churn.

Dropping more bombs

AFTER I GOT BACK HOME FROM THE BIKING WEEKEND, I stayed very quiet about all that had gone on. I went to work. I went to the gym. I got ready to head back to school in the fall. I was very vested in keeping the biking weekend for *myself.* I didn't want to spoil the fantasy in which Jack and I had lived, even though it was just for a couple of days.

Jack began to reach out to me. He called me when his dog passed away. He was coming near our hometown for work and asked to see me. My parents were heading out of town for their annual state fair trip. It should come as no surprise that Jack's working dates coincided with the departure of my parents. They knew he was coming in to visit and seemed fine with it, or at least gave that impression.

Jack arrived and swept me away for the day for a local tourist train ride and some general walking around. Fantasy secured, for now.

He spent the night with me at my (empty) parents' house where an evening of sex and snuggling were the main events. He left the next day and we talked about trying to see each other more frequently after I went away again to school. We felt quite in love by that point and it was clear the love train was stopping for no amount of family wounding that was to come once everyone found out about us.

When Jack and I decided that what was between us was the "real deal" and something both of us wanted to continue, I found myself in the position of lone truth-teller all over again — out in the open by myself. Very convenient that the other adult in collusion with me didn't have to do very much adulting. Jack was able to stay safely insulated from the explosion of the next emotional bomb about to be dropped.

When my mom and dad got back from the state fair, I psyched myself up, sat them both down, and told them Jack and I had begun a relationship.

Their reaction was quite different this time around. I don't think my news was much of a surprise, but I think my mom for sure just didn't want to believe this was happening — *again*. She seemed to simmer and simmer on something, and then, I think it was late the same night I dropped the bomb on them, she told me she and Jack had slept together before she married my dad.

Let's allow this information to sink in. My mom had kept a years-long, somewhat close friendship with a former intimate partner, and then he slept with her daughter too. By the time I found out about her and Jack, I was already up to my neck in the fantasy of Jack and I. There was no way I was going to leave all the amazing treatment, attention, and validation I got from him right then, so I went straight to denial that Jack had ever had sex with her in order to make it okay to stay with him.

I want to take a moment here to offer my mother some grace. I have a hard time imagining how this pill was supposed to go down for her. I feel strongly that her own need for nurturing, attention, and validation were the things that silenced her voice at times when she wanted to speak up and also made her think she wanted or needed people like Jack or Bryan around her.

Denial is a very attractive friend when we are faced with what seems like insurmountable shame. It allowed me to go right on receiving the trauma-wrapped-in-a-big-warm-hug that Jack was serving up. Denial allowed my mother to silence herself and to choose risky people who were allowed near our family. If it were me in the same role as her when she found out about Jack and me — today I have a teenage daughter myself — I probably would have seriously contemplated finding a tall building off of which to jump.

Sometimes the only option for survival and resilience in the face of such wounding is to compartmentalize the shit out of a thing until it feels like it's gone. The wound never heals and the festering may reach a breaking point, but not immediately, at least, and we can all pretend that everything is okay for a moment.

There is no limit to the helpings of trauma soup one receives in life when the first wounds are not intentionally healed. The Universe keeps serving up whatever it is we need to assist us in learning or to force us closer to eventual rock-bottom and surrender. Of course the same scenario would continue to repeat itself until I (and she) was willing to do the work of healing the original rape trauma. Rock bottom was still a few years way for me, but the slope was getting steeper.

The drive with my parents back to college in Iowa was tense. I unloaded my stuff into my dorm and they left without ceremony. I wondered if they were happy to be free of me for a time. I have no doubt that my behavior was baffling and exasperating to my parents, to say the least. The break felt good for me too, and that was the end of the last summer I ever spent at home.

The weird year of Jack

MY SCHOOL CALENDAR WAS SET UP in such a way as to offer "intensive" course study. Students would immerse themselves in one class, all day, every day for three-and-a-half weeks (a "block") and then have a four day reprieve (a "block break") before the next intensive class began. Even though Jack was several hours away in northern Minnesota, it was pretty easy to maintain a relationship given all this free time each month. He would travel down to me, or I would find a ride with other students to go up and stay with him during each block break.

We had a good time during those breaks. We played outside a lot — hiking, hunting, boating, biking, cross-country ski, snowshoeing. He was quite a Grizzly Adams type of guy. And, so nurturing I just couldn't get enough of the red carpet he would roll out when we were together.

Right from the start of these block break visits, I had a really hard time having sex with him — *performing*, sex in general had become all *performance* for me by then. The first nights of our visits I would shut down and pull into myself for a while, as a way to build myself up and "prepare" for sex on the following days.

I was attracted to Jack, but I think I was starting to feel the trade-off I was constantly making: giving away sex for love, care, and nurturing. If I could have a minute to myself to put on my armor and then be the one in charge of the decision to be sexual, I could then *make it work*.

One should not have to *make sex work*. That was one of the effects of the earlier rape I had experienced — *making sex work at the implied or spoken request/demand of another,* even if no physical power exchange takes place. This *performance* repeated on each visit, and became the beginning of the end before long.

Toward springtime of that school year, Jack was getting pretty serious about me. One day we were lounging on his couch, and he jokingly/seriously asked "You want to get married?" I must have looked petrified, because he immediately recovered and said "Wow, you should have seen the look on your face!" I feel certain that if I would have said yes, he would have been on the phone to schedule the Justice of the Peace before I could have said *"camouflage wedding gown"*.

Knowing what Jack ultimately wanted with me, I started to pull away. Rather than just breaking up with Jack on the level (*I needed to keep my fantasy/nurturing bases covered in order to keep running from my trauma*), I started seeing someone else at school and lying to Jack about it. Shame, shame, and more shame. I could not seem to just be on my own. In order to have the strength to leave one shitty sexual relationship trade-off, I needed to have another one to run *toward*.

Born to run

I MANAGED TO KEEP THESE TWO SEXUAL "PLATES" SPINNING in the air for several months while negotiating my first of many "geographical solutions." I decided to transfer schools to the University of Wisconsin, Eau Claire.

The small private school I had been attending was becoming increasingly expensive and I needed a degree option that wasn't going to leave me in a mountain of student loan debt. Plus, I was ready for something different — I was trying to leave behind some pain and shame and hopefully gain a fresh start. I would soon find out that until I did the healing work that trauma demands, I might as well have packed an extra bag for all my demons, because they were moving to Wisconsin right along with me whether I wanted them to or not.

I bought my first car, loaded it up with everything I owned, and hit the road with $50 in my pocket, a friend's guest bed upon which to crash near Eau Claire, and a self-imposed, three-day deadline to find a job and an affordable apartment.

I arrived at my friend's place, got a good night's sleep, and by the end of the next day I had a job at the local hardware store and a 200-square-foot studio apartment — all for myself. I think this was the first step I had ever taken in defining something I truly wanted. I wanted independence, and badly.

I have such gratitude for the way I made this move — I was able to show myself how much I could truly do with a little faith in myself, the Universe, and hard work — three gifts that would save me many times over in the coming years, and that still bail me out on the regular today.

I loved so much making my little space a reflection of who I was. I cut out some artwork for the walls from old wrapping paper, alphabetized my music collection, bought and cooked the food I wanted, and practiced scratching out a self-guided existence during the summer before my classes started at the U.

Jack was still in the picture when I first came to Eau Claire, and had helped me to move some things into my new space. He then got busy doing things like buying me groceries and other sundries. All of a sudden, I saw that his nurturing was really more parenting, and that did *not* feel good. I was quickly falling out of love with him, and managed to tell him so before he left on that first move-in weekend.

Not that any of my breakups were ever quick or easy. In addition to my meeting and hooking up with several random (and still much older) men, Jack and I continued to see each other on and off for the remainder of the summer. Each visit got a bit more cloying and a lot less enjoyable. It was finally completely over in late August before my junior year of college began.

We do what we know

ONE OF THE RANDOM MEN I "FOUND" that summer was a former youth pastor: Jeffrey.

Jeffrey had been my youth leader at church when I was around 14 and 15 years old. He was a charismatic 1970's/groovy kind of guy. He was a breath of fresh air in our boring Methodist youth program and our whole group liked him a lot. I even got to be part of the adult hiring committee who interviewed him. He remembered the names of the whole panel on the first try, which I thought was amazing.

Jeffrey planned fun activities for our group and took the confirmation kids to Washington DC all the years he worked at the church. We had lock-ins. We sang songs. We talked about God and spirituality and being allowed to question things and different ways to form our own ideas about faith and religion. I never knew church employees could also be fun, playful, and, well, *cool*.

Jeffery left the church after 2 or 3 years. I believe there was a question about his behavior with one of the parishioners, and I can even remember my mom being upset about it and questioning out loud the validity of the complaint from the (female) church member.

By this time, Jeffery had also become a trusted family friend. He lived near us. He hung out at our house and came to dinner parties somewhat regularly. I cleaned his house for spending money. He even officiated at my sister's wedding.

After he left the church, he stayed connected with our family for a time, and then ended up moving back to his hometown near his children. He continued to send letters to me throughout college. When I was home, I met up with him on a couple of occasions at state parks for hiking. I remember one such hike where he spoke of a former relationship and went into vivid detail about how the sex was in that relationship. I felt uncomfortable, but listened anyway, again not knowing I even had the choice to say things like "This is gross. I don't want to hear about this."

When I moved to Eau Claire that first summer, I reached out to him out of loneliness to see if he wanted to meet up in Minneapolis for another hike. We did.

During that hike, we talked like we had on previous occasions about any little thing. And then after a while, there we were making out on a park bench. Again, being swept up in the moment, again, wondering afterward "what the hell just happened?" And feeling grossed out about it on the drive back to my apartment. I struggle to remember who started the kissing, and I go back and forth with self-blame as I remember the whole scenario. He wrote me a couple more letters and I think we met one more time after that, but with no kissing on that occasion. It was just awkward and weird and not a little slimy. Plus that age thing again — he was older, even, than Jack. Ugh.

I debated including Jeffrey in the narrative because what happened between us seemed kind of small when I first thought about it, but I decided to put it in because it speaks to pattern, and also to access. Jeffrey was given access to me as a young teenager by my church and also by my parents, who befriended him outside of church. He was another older man who just seemed to "hang out" with our family, and therefore with me. I had occasion to be around him on many youth group trips, and my parents also gave permission for him to take my and one of my friends on an overnight camping trip all by ourselves. He let us drive when we were underage on the campground roads. This might seem inconsequential, but right there is another example of the kind of "secrets" these people like to hand out and then hold over their victims.

My friend and I escaped any kind of molestation that trip, but I implore the reader to notice the extreme risk my parents took by allowing a single man in a position of influence (church youth pastor) such easy access to alone time with their daughter. And, by setting this example early on, they created instances like this as "normal," which means I would have a higher chance of minimizing a violation if it occurred, as well as repeating this risky behavior with my children as well.

Can we see now how molestation/assault/harassment becomes acceptable? Especially if we have kids, it behooves us to take a long look at the people we allow around our family and the situations into which we place our kids. I can look back and see several instances where I may have placed Blaire at risk out of sheer need for care for her when I was a single mom, or even just my own naiveté. There are plenty of ways to be open and generally trusting and not live in fear all the time, but also to take some simple steps to guard your kids against situations where they are asked to handle things that no child should have to handle. One of those ways is to not allow your kids to be anywhere alone with activity/group leaders, male or female. This protects both the child and the adult from being placed in questionable circumstances. When enrolling your child in an activity, it pays to ask whether staff have been given any kind of child abuse prevention training. I did receive that training in my workplace years later, and that was actually how I found out that many of the things Jeffery was doing with me, though not classified as molestation, were highly inappropriate and should never have been allowed to happen. Now back to that first summer in Eau Claire...

True to form, I couldn't get beyond that fact that without Jack, I would be *alone* and without a reliable source of validation and attention. It would be more than a decade before I learned that *I* was the one who needed to be the source of those things for me, so instead, I made a fateful phone call. Enter Bryan, The Sequel.

Bryan, the sequel:
Or the complete absorption of the woman once known as Leah

E VEN THOUGH THE MOVE TO WISCONSIN was ultimately good for me in many ways, the first bit of time I spent there was really hard. I worked several jobs to make ends meet, and I still had no money, like most college students.

Instead of trying to grow real friendships with women in this new town, I fulfilled all my social needs by going to the local bar (underage, no less) and finding older men with whom to hook up. It was what I knew and it was so easy. Though I was never physically harmed in the process of these hook-ups, I took many risks with complete strangers. I'm very lucky that the worst did not happen that summer.

In a weak and lonely moment, and because I still knew his number, I called Bryan. Just to talk. That's what I told myself. Not only did we talk, but everything that had captivated me about him when I was 15 was completely rekindled. He appeared to be having a good time too, and a few conversations later he made plans to drive up for a few days to see my new digs and reconnect. He seemed happy to be able to squeeze in a late-summer vacation and had always enjoyed that part of the world.

This visit was under the guise of "friendship." I will never know if he was intentionally laying the groundwork for what was to happen next, or if his opportunistic streak kicked in once more after we met up.

At any rate, he drove up and we spent the weekend together. Once he got to my apartment, all of the same attraction came rushing back. I was instantly hooked in again to his powerful vibe — it was like I was 15 still, and gazing at him on the porch in the rain. I'm sure that my attraction was an epic boost to his (already oversized) ego, and he got off on that to a high degree.

Once the ice-breaking formalities were out of the way, we pretty much spent the whole weekend in bed together. This time around, I knew more about my own body and so much more about how to *perform*. Even though much later I could see this *performing* for what it was — a cry for help and a bid to fill an ever-widening hole in myself — at the time, the *performance* felt wildly intense and addictive. I wanted more. Now it was actually the sex that had a new tug on my spirit, my body, and my brain. Bryan would see this and use it expertly for the means to his ends soon enough.

A funny thing about trauma is that it serves to halt our emotional growth until we seek help and do the work we need to do to heal the wounds. So, if we are traumatized, especially sexually/relationally, we maintain the same maturity level that we had at the time of the trauma even though we still age chronologically. It is the same with alcoholism or drug addiction — emotional growth halts when the addiction begins.

When Bryan came to see me again, it was a huge trigger for 15-year-old me and that is how I always related to him — as a 15-year-old girl captivated by a romantic fantasy, in a rape-culture upbringing, from an attractive older man who had power and means. Because he lived so far away, the distance served to cement the fantasy. I never was close enough to get to know the real, everyday Bryan. I believe if I had known that part of him I may have woken up from my trauma trance a lot sooner and found the power to tell him goodbye. Alas, that was not my path.

After he left, there was another hole to fill. Bryan and I had not spoken of beginning a new relationship — the weekend he spent seemed to stand on its own. However, we began to call each other with growing regularity, and our conversations were getting deep and emotional very fast. I was still continuing to see other men casually as autumn wore on, and he was still loosely involved with the same woman from several years before, but we were beginning to discuss the option to be exclusively and officially together.

A fate-sealing trip

B Y THIS POINT IN THE STORY I AM TIRED. *I feel like a guest on a very bad talk show who has gone way beyond her allotted 15 minutes. I wish I were not the owner of this story. I wish I were not the owner of the feelings I feel when I write it.*

My story is so... tedious? I was not kidnapped and held prisoner for years — at least not in the strictly physical sense. I was not trafficked. I was not drugged in a bar and then jumped in an alley. Maybe trauma is somehow perversely easier to define and heal if it is more violent and truly torturous. Those are the stories that deserve books, documentaries, and 20-years-later-where-are-they-now TV shows. I don't feel like my story should have a whole book about it, and yet, I have more to say.

The only reason to keep writing the words, I think, is that maybe I'm not alone. Maybe other women have grown up in a similar soup and are wondering why they shut down during sex, leave their bodies and live in their heads, always find the most destructive and abusive partners, use chemicals to get numb, or even simply feel disgusting if a man whistles at them on the street or shoots a leering stare their way at the office.

"What is wrong with me?" we ask ourselves. "Why can't I just be normal? Why is true intimacy so fucking hard?" "Why is it easier to perform instead of feel my sexuality?" I hope that as I continue to write maybe a door can open on some answers to those questions, and we can all finally believe the fact that there is nothing wrong with us.

Instead, there is everything wrong with a culture that rewards both men and women for staying quiet, staying passive, staying permissive, laughing it off, and staying victims when sex is monetized, marginalized, debased, dumbed down, and used as a violent tool for powerful gain. We must all start using our voices for current rape culture to change. Those voices must all begin by telling the truth. May all our stories be brought into the light and transmuted into powerful tools for change. We are only as sick as our secrets.

Bryan and I got deeper and deeper into connection/obsession over the phone through autumn and into winter. We were keen to see each other again, and rather than him visiting the northland during snow season, a trip to meet in New Orleans was planned. Since I had no money, he of course paid for everything from the plane tickets to the swanky hotel to the food and attractions. I had no idea then how much I would eventually have to "pay" for all this generosity.

We arrived in the Big Easy on a brisk January evening. We got to the hotel — a beautiful historic building in the French Quarter that had been a feature in several films over the years. I was head-over-heels in fantasy and drunk on the romance of being with powerful, wealthy Bryan in such a picturesque scene.

We headed up to the room, and after the build-up and anticipation of travelling, we went straight to sex. Again, the romance intensified the sensations, and I was eager to act out my part. After coming down a bit from the physical high of coming together again, Bryan and I hit the town.

The rest of the week proceeded in similar fashion — wake up each morning in a sunny, infatuated haze, stumble out of the hotel for breakfast and sightseeing, back to the hotel for afternoon sex, out on the town for drinking and more intrigue, and then more sex after that. It was during this trip that Bryan began grooming me for his kink side: Bondage and Discipline.

Into the kink world, for worse

I T BEGAN WITH A CHOKER — necklace, that is. I happened to have one that I wore because they were fashionable at that moment — it was a black crocheted choker with a small fabric rose in front. Bryan mentioned he thought they were very sexy, and that I looked great in that sort of jewelry.

This seemed harmless enough. He had mentioned several months earlier that he had a proclivity for bondage and discipline during sex. This is where one partner typically restrains the other in some way with rope or scarves or straps and the like, and then might deliver "punishment" in both verbal and physical form. This kink is all about power exchange, with one partner usually playing the dominant while the other plays the submissive.

When he first told me about it, I thought it was quite comical, and I couldn't understand the allure or arousal from such nonsense. Knowing that Bryan thought I would look beautiful in a choker, though, I could get my head around that. I wanted to be "perfect" for him — everything he wanted so that he would never take away his attention and favor — my two drugs of choice. The lacy choker necklace was very feminine and romantic. He was pleased when I wore it during that trip and told me so. And so it went, for a time — the grooming continued.

During his next visit to my apartment a couple of months later, he brought "things." A chain for my waist, a collar that closed with a padlock he had wrapped up like a present for me to open.

These items scared me when I saw them, and I did not want to have them as part of our sexual experience. I wondered why we could not just have normal sex — why that (read, "I") was not enough for him.

Bryan patted down my fears by telling me we could stop at any time, that we had already discovered we could have good sex with just us and we could always go back and do that. He told me that this kind of "play" was a symbol of great trust between the two of us and he didn't take it lightly. He said it was a way for powerful, assertive women like myself to feel that I could truly "let go". Wanting so badly to please him, and hearing him say how important this was to him, I reluctantly said "okay" as I allowed him to lock the collar around my neck and the heavy chain around my waist.

I wasn't sure quite what to expect next, but Bryan led the way, as always. This kink behavior was a pattern for him, and I was just the next opportunity for him to demonstrate his cunning and power.

Bryan started asking me to respond to him during sex verbally in specific ways. He would ask me a question, and I would have to respond with "I am your perfect slave," or "You are my perfect master." He would bind my hands with a scarf, or put a chain around my waist while penetrating me or while we exchanged oral sex. He always placed a collar on my neck. I had to have his permission before having an orgasm, and to verbally say that my orgasms were always "for him."

Deep breath. I have walled off these details for some time, and writing about them brings up shame and embarrassment, as well as more knots in my stomach and bile in my throat. I have courage, though, that I am not alone in these feelings or the experience of this type of gradual, manipulative violation. I've learned the only way I (or anyone else) can heal this kind of shame is by telling the truth, feeling the emotions and the grief, and moving through to some new place on the "other side."

An element that I have a hard time talking about is how *intensely arousing* this kind of sex felt. That fact has been a really confusing one to admit. The heat of the physical/sexual sensation was turned up all the way during these events. And, even though he would say that we could go back to the way sex began with us, once he had introduced his kink preferences, we never *did* have sex again without him needing to have some kind of dominance over me.

So, I was "allowed" all this physical pleasure, but never a position of equality in the relationship. I had been so damaged already through the past five years I had no idea this wasn't a healthy way to conduct a real partnership; that in order for there to be a power exchange, both partners have to have power to begin with. That wasn't the case here. I also did not know yet that I had a voice to speak up against a 43-year-old man who held all the cards.

Perhaps there are some readers out there who are well-versed in the kink or bondage and discipline world. Certainly, books and clubs and movies like Fifty Shades of Grey *have promoted this type of sexual activity as erotic, titillating, and glamorous.*

For those people who act out their kinks as informed, consensual adults without any sexual wounding in their pasts, I would be hard-pressed to pass judgement. As for me, and others who may have experienced trauma as a result of kink- or fetish-based sex, I maintain that because of my young age, and the genesis of my involvement with Bryan, this type, or any type, of sex with him was never consensual, always manipulative, and consistently a bid from him to gain more power over my whole life, not just my body and the sex we had. Therefore, it was a violation many times over and rape is what I call it.

As winter turned to spring that same year, Bryan kept up the intensity. He was home in Atlanta while I was finishing up the school year in Wisconsin. We spoke on the phone most evenings, often with him leading me down a list of items for sexual "preparation" and then phone sex. He continued to make particular demands even from a distance.

In his letters, he used fantasy scenarios about us to flesh out the details of his kink preferences. Those preferences began to include a desire for me to experience pain. He even stated in one letter that "good" submissives learned how to climax at times from pain rather than pleasure. This idea really freaked me out, and I told him so. I was not sure what to do. Internally, I wondered when it would be enough. When would he reach a level place with sex that didn't change? That I could count on and feel secure with? He assured me again that this was a new frontier of trust we were embarking upon and that he would never take it "too far." ("By whose definition?" I wondered.)

I read this last bit through and made a few grammar edits and spell-checks, and I wondered where my family was during this time. They knew that Bryan was back in my life, and I think I isolated myself intentionally because of all the shame I felt about how much pain I knew I was probably causing for them.

We all did several "surface" kinds of things together — Thanksgiving, Christmas, a short ski-trip with my dad, but the family bonds were definitely chilly during this time. When I told them that winter that Bryan and I were starting to get serious and that I was planning both a spring and summer trip to his home, they pretty much divorced themselves from me for a time. Or at least that is what I assumed. I was too afraid of the pain of connecting with them and too afraid of the pain of losing Bryan (or rather, the attention and favor that I constantly had to work harder to win) to do anything but keep running back to the easiest place — the fantasy and the sex and the lifestyle that Bryan was promising me.

Spring break rolled around and Bryan bought a ticket for me to travel to Atlanta for the week. This would be the first time I ever saw his home, met his family, or discovered what "real life Bryan" was like. I was excited and more than a little nervous about how the week would transpire.

Bryan and his family welcomed me with open arms. Both Bryan and his brother Kent lived in a sprawling ranch-style southern home, along with their late-stage-Alzheimer's mother and a live-in nurse.

From a distance, the week looked promising. I got to know Atlanta a little bit, I helped out with a few house projects, and Bryan made time for some sightseeing adventures for us as well. All of the non-sexual activities were still enough, then, to offset my growing sense of discomfort around the sex and the new demands Bryan was continuing to make.

Now that we were in Bryan's home for this visit, he used the opportunity to bring out more of his B and D "equipment". There were whips, riding crops, and more bondage straps and collars. He was also seeming to get off more on making me verbalize my devotion to him as my "perfect master." I believe the height of his arousal came from my willingness to place myself so far beneath him — he would always look for ways to cement the roles we each played. The power exchange we were in only got more pronounced as time went on.

That one summer where I nearly ceased to exist

S INCE THE SPRING BREAK TRIP WENT RELATIVELY WELL, Bryan and I began talking about how I could come down there for the entire summer. I needed to find a job in Atlanta and get my apartment and car buttoned up for the season.

Through a family connection, Bryan got me an interview for an internship position with the Atlanta Chamber of Commerce. It was an easy job to land and actually looked like fun — stuffing envelopes and answering phones by day, helping to host business networking events by night at several swanky Atlanta locales. I packed up all my clothes, locked up the Wisconsin apartment for three months, and headed to my new southern summer home.

The first month was pretty amazing. I was able to finally have the fantasy of "playing house" with Bryan. I went to sleep and woke up with him every day. We had our breakfast together and he would drop me off at the train station on his way to work. I liked getting to know my new job (my first "adult" job that did not involve bartending, selling concessions, or giving tours) and I got along well with the other interns who were also all college students. I even had the chance to teach a couple of fitness classes at a gym close to the office, an activity I had enjoyed since age 17.

I loved Atlanta — so different from Wisconsin with new and diverse people, a whole new language (all sodas were "Coke," every person was "y'all"), and Soul Food — it was exciting to be in a new cultural mix. Bryan introduced me to a few of his coworkers and neighbors, and seemed proud and happy to have me so close.

I began to find out that every-day-Bryan was nothing out of the ordinary. He was a loner and homebody and liked to visit the hardware store and work on house projects on the weekends. He was a movie buff. We did normal couples things like dinner, hiking, house/yard work, a concert, a neighborhood barbeque. These activities and connections felt good to me — the illusion of stable family life and so much of what I had been seeking for so long. If only keeping this life didn't cost me so much.

On the flip side of this ho-hum suburban life, there was a big secret that Bryan and I hid from the world down in his basement bedroom. He continued to push the envelope with each "session." (He no longer called what we did "sex" or "making love" — looking back that was because what we did was no longer sex — it was physical intensity and power exchange.)

My bindings became more elaborate, now to include different types of gags for my mouth — a ball gag, a phallic gag — the cherry on top of the domination sundae being the literal silencing of my voice. Now, I was reduced to moaning and drooling while he did sexual things to me as I was bound to the bed — the fear I was feeling supposedly enhancing the "trust and bonding" between us.

The low point for me was finding myself standing on tip toes in high spike heels, gagged (I think, this is such a hard memory that all of the details are not quite clear), arms stretched and shackled overhead, dangling by a chain from a ceiling beam. This while he stroked my body, held a crop in his hand, and told me how beautiful I looked. I was so beside myself with shame, embarrassment, and fear. I got his attention enough for him to release my mouth. "Please take me down," I said, on the verge of tears.

After a moment, he released me and walked me back to the bedroom. I don't remember what happened next, if we continued with the "session," or if we stopped for that day.

I am tempted to minimize this story. I don't want to believe that it (still) has such an effect on me. I began to describe these events in a therapy group several years ago, and before I got all the way through, one woman had to leave the room because she felt too uncomfortable to stay.

It is a scene that has been described many times in erotic literature or played out in soft and hard-core pornography movies (Fifty Shades of Grey again comes to mind.) Maybe there are readers out there who are thinking "That wasn't so bad — what is she whining about? Plus, she signed up for the whole thing in the first place." My fear is that anyone reading this account will think those thoughts. My guess is that many women feel this way about reporting their rapes, so they remain silent.

I can remember today what the ball gag felt like whenever he used it — messy with drool, uncomfortably stretching my mouth, making it impossible to do anything but moan, reducing me to a mute animal — all for the gratification of a man who claimed to love me, to revere me, to value me, to favor me, to not leave marks on me.

The marks Bryan left were never visible. I could feel the marks on the inside and I was beginning to see the awful mess I was in. All the orgasms in the world could not balance the fact that I was being lost — co-opted in the worst possible way — by being made to believe this power exchange was all my choice.

I was isolated from family and friends in what might as well have been another country. I was financially and emotionally dependent on this man. I had over a month until my plane ride back to school, and no idea that there may have been other options. Leaving early seemed impossible because I had no job to go back to, plus I owed Bryan some money for expenses like business clothing, and he was keeping my paychecks in his bank account for "convenience".

I was afraid to call my parents because I felt sure they couldn't or wouldn't help, and I was still so ashamed of the entire situation that I did not want to risk their further disappointment in me. I was 21 years old. He was 44. I was trapped.

Near the end of July, I drove myself into work one morning. I was frustrated with traffic, and at one intersection, rolled down my window, flipped the bird to an "offending" car, and screamed at the driver as loud as I could. I had to pull over to calm down, so wound up was I.

That was my wake-up call — that seemingly small moment on the road. I knew I was not the person who raged at drivers with their windows rolled up. I turned my car around, headed back to the house, and called in sick to work. Nothing was physically wrong, so to speak, but I felt like I needed a timeout. My boss was fine with my absence... it was the only such day I asked for during the entire internship.

I took the dog and headed to a nearby nature area with some hiking trails. After a few hours outside on my own, I felt better. I felt like I could breathe again, and that tomorrow would be okay. Of course there was more brewing here than I realized, but it was enough for that day to make a small decision for myself.

I met Bryan at the house later, and he was *not* pleased. I got the silent treatment and the cold shoulder — two things I had never imagined would happen. He appeared to be really angry that I had not gone into work that day, but he would not talk to me about *anything*. I. Was. Devastated. This kind of pull-back made me feel like all my insides were being ripped out. I was panicked and grief-stricken and physically sick.

The silence persisted for a full week. The only exchanges we had during that time were daily task-related. I couldn't sleep in the same bed with him while he was so frosty without knowing what happened to make him so angry, so I moved into the guest room for a couple of nights.

Since I had *no one* to talk to and could not figure out what I had done that was so wrong, I broke down and called my parents. Bryan had taken away completely the two things that were like air to me — his approval and his attention. Being essentially 15 years old in a 21-year-old body, I could not see this for what it was — a grown man having a temper tantrum at the loss, even in a small way, of power over his favorite plaything.

That week, I felt almost exactly the same as I had on the couch with my parents when they first found out about Bryan and I. Again I found myself on an island of grief and loss and uncertainty and abject sadness, with no option for redemption, it seemed.

My parents did the best they could from far away to comfort me and help me through those days. I am grateful for that. Sometimes I wish they would have come down to rescue me, but then I'm not sure if I would have allowed them to take me away. Maybe some challenges are better faced alone.

Bryan slowly began to thaw out after that week went by, but something had changed. Maybe something in him — I guess I hurt him or disillusioned him or something with my little decision to take a solo walk in the woods, because he seemed to maintain a touch of sterility and distance from that point forward.

As for me, I began to shift. I started getting tired of the power exchange. I suggested to Bryan that he was pissed off because I had done something perfectly in keeping with where I was at that moment: I behaved exactly like a college student. He didn't disagree. I was starting to want things for myself; chief among them to be liked for who I was and not the performances I could give.

I think I strapped on some virtual armor for the last few weeks of my stay. Bryan and I continued to have "sessions," though less frequently and with less intensity. I started leaving my body during these sessions — I would numb out and just try to go somewhere else in my head. So much was my bodily desertion that I stopped responding to him physically when he had me bound up and/or gagged, which frustrated him. I even remember him saying "Come for me, bitch!" when my body was limp while he was performing oral sex on me. That statement shocked me into an orgasm, and then it could all be over until next time.

I think Bryan needed a willing participant in the submission for his own arousal, so the exchange was no longer as satisfying for him. He left me alone more. Even though I could not yet use my voice to simply tell him "*No!*" my body took over and found a way to help me get out. Such is the way with trauma.

As the start of my senior year neared, I was looking very much forward to getting back to my Wisconsin home. Bryan still had some triggering "hooks" in me, however, and I asked if he would accompany me back home to help me get re-settled in. He made it into a family vacation of sorts, and Bryan and I ended up flying back up north to spend a few days in Minneapolis with one of his old friends, and then Bryan's brother Kent met the three of us at the Minnesota State Fair. After that, Bryan planned to drive me the short distance over the state line to Eau Claire.

That last night we spent in Minneapolis, we had sex one last time. Though there was no "equipment" for him to use, he was still trying to wield power over me with his demands for my verbal confirmation of his role as my Perfect Master and me as his Perfect Slave. I said the words, but they were hollow for me — a necessary formality to get through before being able to do regular stuff like going to the fair. I just wanted it all to be over, and that seemed to be the quickest and easiest way to make it happen. He drove me home after the fair with promises to call and wishes for me to enjoy the start of school. And then he left. I never saw him again.

Courage to leave,
but not to change

I BEGAN SCHOOL WITH LITTLE FANFARE. My classes were engaging and enjoyable, and I had gotten a new job as an after-school nanny for a family near campus. Bryan and I were still talking several times per week, but I was getting back into my own life and expanding on it some. I started going out again to dance at my favorite local bar and I began meeting new people. One of those people was a man named James.

James asked me to two-step on a couple of occasions, and I found out he was a good dancer. A mutual friend kept saying we should go over to a suburb of St. Paul, Minneapolis, (about an hour's drive away) where there was a larger country dance bar with a bigger floor and a better mix of music. James and I made plans to head over one weekend "as friends."

Bryan was still calling me often, but I was getting tired of his continued attempts to control me. I even laughed out loud one time at a message he left on my answering machine about him being disappointed I was not in when he called, and that that wasn't how a proper slave treated her master. I watched myself wake up in that moment to the absolute absurdity of the whole power exchange between us. I was so grateful I did not live closer to him... it seemed what I needed in order to see the forest for the trees was a little distance.

Though distance was enough for me to find the courage and the voice to leave, the residual effects of the original trauma were far from healed. True to form, I still needed to be able to run toward another (equally damaging, it would turn out) relationship to leave the shitty one I was still kind of in. James was the man I ran toward.

James was nice enough without coming off as particularly charming. He was good-looking and seemed to have most of his shit together. He was 15 years older than me, a former sailor in the Navy, and worked for a large computer parts company in Eau Claire. He had moved to town within the last year from South Dakota, had been out of a previous marriage for a couple of years, and seemed to enjoy the fresh start his company offered him when he was transferred to Wisconsin.

A couple of weekends after those first few two-steps, James and I went to the Twin Cities for a fun evening of dancing. Initially, the evening was casual. We chatted amicably on the drive to the club and sat with a larger group of acquaintances once we arrived. I had plenty of dance partners and so did he, but he seemed to want to watch out for me a bit as well, making sure I was safe if I went outside for fresh air, or checking to see if my drinks needed refilling.

Toward the end of the evening we were slow dancing together, and I was making it clear I was up for being more than friends.

I must have been terrified of being "alone." I couldn't seem to figure out yet how to be my own source of companionship, affirmation, acceptance and love. Here came another opportunity to run away from what I could not recognize, define, or understand — the pain and scars of sexual trauma. I would repeat this behavior of seeking out intrigue, romance, and secrecy until years later when I finally asked for help.

"Living in the extremes" is one hallmark symptom of unresolved trauma. Many trauma survivors search for ways to repeat elements of their trauma, or at least ways to keep experiencing the adrenaline rush or the addictive brain chemicals (adrenaline, norepinephrine, serotonin, dopamine) that accompany a state of high arousal. This aroused state could be sexual, fear/thrill/risk, or attachment, or something else. Especially in prolonged trauma like mine, it seemed that my normal state was one of high arousal and vigilance (making sure I was always in "pleasing" mode — vigilant for mood/behavior changes in others.) If those two things were not present, I felt like something was wrong — I had to relearn how to be okay in a relaxed or simply contented mental and emotional place.

James drove me home, and I invited him inside for a drink. After a bit of a chat, we got closer and closer until we were kissing. He ended up spending the night, though we did not have sex. He left after breakfast the next morning with promises to call soon. Sometime during all the late-night canoodling, I heard a voice in my head clearly state "You are going to marry this man." Today, I believe that was my trauma voice.

At this point I was still attached, at least by phone, to Bryan. James was also dating a couple of women very casually, but as soon as all this "passion" erupted between the two of us, we agreed to date exclusively and sever romantic ties with our respective entanglements. I called Bryan a few days later to tell him I had met someone else. He hung up on me. I never heard from him again. It took what it took, but I was free from him, or so it seemed for a few shining moments.

The relationship ramped up quickly for James and me. I moved in with him about three months after we met, and in another three months, we were engaged. My relationship theme never seemed to wear out — since I couldn't see yet how to provide for my *own* emotional and validational (is that a word?) needs, I kept looking outside myself for someone to care for me in that way. It was always a tradeoff for sex, though it may have felt a lot like love at the time. Remember, when a person experiences trauma, unless they seek out intervention, support, and healthy coping tools, all real emotional growth stops. Even though I appeared to be a somewhat competent young adult in many ways, I was still emotionally and spiritually a 15-year-old looking for a romantic fantasy. Fantasy was, in fact, the *only* thing I could attract.

James had been open about the fact that he was a former drug addict and alcoholic who had survived an abusive childhood. He had been sober from prescription painkillers for several years and from alcohol for over a decade. He also had recently quit smoking, was exercising regularly at his workplace fitness center, and seemed to be somewhat health-conscious. I think I met him at his absolute best. I think he probably met me at my absolute worst.

Often, trauma survivors will find each other in large crowds of otherwise healthy people — we seem to have some kind of antennae for people who are equally wounded and scarred, and we choose those people to partner up with because they are like us. It's only a matter of time before one partner triggers the other, and then, unfortunately, it is all downhill from there, many times for both people. With me and James, I was the first one to implode.

Even though I felt sure I wanted to marry James and was happy co-habitating during our engagement, our life got very regular after that initial whirlwind courtship. "Regular" never lasted very long with me then. Several months after we were engaged, he applied for a new job working as a traveling manufacturing consultant with a dramatically higher paycheck. He got the job as well as the schedule — 12 days on the road and every other weekend home. All of a sudden, I found myself alone again — a lot.

With all my free time, I began going out at night on my own. I didn't have any close female friends with which to do other things, so I went to that same bar in town (where James and I had been going regularly, still, since we began dating) as well as the one down the road an hour in the Twin Cities. I was a good dancer in a provocative wardrobe so I got a lot of (sexual) attention from men whenever I would go out to dance. That attention felt so good to me that it was only a matter of time before the attention turned into more.

There were two random men that summer and fall who I hooked up with — one was a mutual friend of James and mine, and the other was a sugar daddy of sorts who was ridiculously older than me. The mutual friend and I had driven to the distant club, and when we got back to his place, he gave me a backrub. I knew he would have been open to sex, but I also knew it was wrong and dishonest so I left abruptly. Not so with the sugar daddy — he and I ended up in my car one evening after dancing exchanging kisses for several minutes before I was able to stop.

Another very common symptom of unresolved sexual trauma is sexual promiscuity. I believe that when women are taught that their only value is sexual, through events like sexual trafficking, molestation, exposure to or involvement in pornography, they (we, I) continue to seek out that same validation even after the trauma is over, because it's all we know. Our current culture enforces this behavior through our use of advertising, our standards of female body perfection, our objectification of women, and our silence about all of the sexual violations accumulating over many generations.

The traumatic symptom of promiscuity can enforce all-too-common victim-blaming rhetoric. "Look at the way she was dressed/was dancing/was making eye contact/was drinking more than she should" are all painfully common statements made to rationalize sexual violence in our society. I have found myself, at times, judging other women in a similar way, even though I, too, was a victim many times over. Lest the reader misunderstand my sentiments about rape victims or the right of a woman to dress, drink, act, dance, or flirt however she chooses, let me be absolutely clear. Rape victims, whether previously traumatized or not, never invite sexual violation with the clothes they wear or the way they behave.

Today, I have pledged to recognize if or when I mentally throw other survivors under the bus by judging their behavior or trying to minimize the culpability of the abuser. In this way, I can turn my judgement into activism, my rationalization into support and unity. My trauma story has an end — a good one. With this narrative, I can use whatever power or clout I may have to speak up for those who have not yet found their own. Change is possible. If one person can change her own life, it is certain a whole society can change as well.

The one hook-up I could not hide

I GRADUATED COLLEGE IN DECEMBER OF 1998. I started school with the intention to become a marine biologist (how I was going to do that in Iowa and Wisconsin, I have no idea), and ended up with a biology major and a music minor. Obviously (?!), I decided to pursue a career in fitness. No, not obviously, but as happens often in college, we study toward our dreams and then end up doing what *pays*. I had been teaching fitness classes starting in high school for pizza and gas money and had really grown to love that kind of work. Plus I had gotten pretty good at it along the way. Immediately after I graduated, I found a full-time job as the Group Fitness Coordinator for the UWEC Recreation department. I was elated at the "grown-up" professional role, as well as the fact that I still had familiar surroundings and a real salary to boot. A perk of the job was being able to go (inexpensively) on Rec Department student trips, one of which was a ski vacation out west to the mountains in Utah. As soon as I found out about this golden opportunity, I signed right up! James was not a skier and was still working his crazy travel schedule anyway, so he stayed behind.

The beginning of the trip was uneventful. A busload of college kids plus a few other extras like myself pulled sleepily into a Salt Lake City hotel after a long drive. We rested up and hit the slopes the next day. One of the other Rec Department managers was also along on the trip, so I hung out with him mostly and several of the students he knew well. One of them was named Brad. He was friendly, talkative, and easy-going. We seemed to connect, and we spent more time together each day of the trip.

As the reader might guess, by the end of the trip, Brad and I had hooked up on several occasions. We went several steps beyond kissing, but had not had sex. One of my rationalizations with all the infidelity was that if I stopped short of sex, it wasn't really that bad and I could sort of pretend I was maintaining some kind of line in the sand. Because this was not just a one-time hook-up with a random person, I couldn't compartmentalize the guilt I felt as well as I had before. Once we got home from the week away, I admitted what I had done to James because I could no longer keep it in and pretend everything was okay.

Moving will fix everything

J AMES WAS *REALLY* ANGRY. I had never seen anyone get quite *that* angry. I remember his face and how screwed up and squinty with rage his eyes looked. I remember him screaming at me while I cowered down in a corner saying "I'm sorry... I'm so sorry," over and over. For a moment, I was a little afraid he might hit me when I saw the news sink in, but instead he did a funny thing. I found out that day that his *own trauma response* was to turn punishment and anger inward toward himself. He went out immediately and bought a pack of cigarettes and smoked them in rapid succession. He did not put them down again for good until years later when a bad car accident gave him new motivation to quit.

The next several days were monumentally hard. I felt remorseful and ashamed. I wanted to stay in the relationship with James, but I don't think I wanted to get married, ultimately. What I really wanted to was to remain in the fantasy of marriage — of stability, of the feeling of acceptance and favor, of the feeling of being taken care of and needed.

Most people in their early 20's are trying to figure out life on their own — they are finding jobs, apartments, and hopefully lively and fulfilling social lives. They are learning to adult. I, on the other hand, wanted to *pretend* to adult by planning a fancy wedding and placing my perfect future husband up there at the very top of our sugar sweet wedding cake. I was trying to create a life of affluent, happy perfection with a man I essentially created in my own mind.

James was doomed from the beginning with me, because I made most of him up in my head and told myself he would live up to all the potential I had given him. I never believed him early on the few times he mentioned he had some pretty big demons in his past. I asked him (at least in my head) to possess a tidy combination of intelligence, wealth, charm, wit, and leadership for this life we were trying to build. I was looking to him to do life for the *both* of us. And then I was angry when *he* didn't deliver everything I had ever thought I wanted. I don't know anyone who can survive very long under that kind of pressure.

Over the next couple of weeks, James and I talked a lot about trust and what our next steps would be. He had interviewed a few weeks earlier for another job that would entail less travel, but a move to Columbus, Ohio. When the offer came in for the job, he took it, and I decided to move with him immediately rather than stay behind until the wedding date. This was my bid to show my commitment to him and to try to get a "fresh start" in a new place.

Sadly for James, I continued to demonstrate that for me, fresh starts were never very fresh because I always took my wounded self with me. The infidelity that I ran away from caught up with me in every new place I moved. Thankfully for me, the hard times came with a few blessings along the way. Perhaps we all have angels who recognize when we need a break for crying out loud.

Columbus proved to be a great town. I was able to find part-time work right away at one of the local YMCAs and also at a large gym near our apartment. I loved living in a big city — the diversity, the energy, the expanded options for things to do, and a momentary shield from anything tempting for me. James and I still had a long way to go before he trusted me again, but I now had a reliable source of intensity and excitement, at least temporarily, because everything around me was brand new. I was okay for the moment and was doing well at my jobs as well as continuing to plan our wedding.

I do, but I didn't

I N THE SPRING OF 1999, James and I still intended to stumble down the aisle together. The invitations went out for our May wedding. The dress was bought, the wedding showers were thrown, the venue, flowers, and cake (two of them — traditional tiered with a little bride and groom at the top surveying the bubbling, simmering cauldron of trauma from which our marriage was birthed, and also a carrot cake with unbelievably rich cream cheese frosting) were secured. The Eau Claire house was up for sale in preparation for finding our permanent house in Columbus. All that was left was to say "I do." We made the drive back to Wisconsin and were set to do the deed on May 22, 1999. I had just turned 23 years old.

I had a great time the morning of my wedding. My family and their friends were all present, (they were so happy I hadn't ended up with Bryan or Jack, they were actually relieved to see me paired off with a divorced, recovering addict 15 years my senior), and my one college buddy had come out from Colorado to be my Maid of Honor. Another old flame from college stood up for me as Bridesman. I got to be the sun, moon, and stars for a whole day, from the massage, hair, and makeup to the pretty dress and the rose petals laid at my feet walking down the aisle.

My father held my arm and together we glided past all the guests there for one reason — to look at and admire *me*. At least, that was the fantasy in which I lived. Once I got to the front of the church, my stomach began to churn. As James said his vows to me, I felt my panic rise under the intensity of his gaze. I felt like he *commanded* his vows to me with a seriousness for which I was completely unprepared. I held his gaze and wanted to throw up. I read my vows and said "I do" in all the right places. I wanted to run but everything was over so fast and then the moment of fear was gone. I could skim right over that panicky instant and head straight to the party — Thank God.

The reception was mostly fun, but also a prelude of things to come with my new in-laws. I had spent time around them here and there during our courtship, but their extreme level of dysfunction together came out during the party. Blows were almost exchanged over an ill-timed practical joke pulled on James and his new truck by his siblings. The event was alarming to say the least, and definitely not part of the wedding day fantasy I had so painstakingly built for myself. Onward, though, ever onward we went, shoving the important stuff aside because it was just too hard and too big to confront and heal — ever, it turned out.

The rest of the wedding weekend was spent opening gifts, thanking everyone for coming, and then packing up the rest of the Eau Claire house to start our married life together back in Columbus. I was rude to my mom when she cried as she and my dad saw us off. I was so ready to *go*. We had one night of a honeymoon at a fancy waterpark resort in Wisconsin Dells, and then we were on the road again. I remember the waterpark feeling so playful, actually, and wanting to prolong that feeling. There was a lot of playing I had missed out on so far — I was a bit sad to cut it short now. Our drive back to Columbus was ordinary and upon returning to Columbus, we resumed life as usual.

The trauma gremlins return

I N THE SUMMER OF 1999, James and I found a house on one acre of land thirty minutes outside of Columbus in the picturesque little town of Granville, Ohio. The house was well-placed on a hill overlooking the town out the front door and a rolling, wooded landscape out the back door. The commute into the workplace was a bit long, but beautiful, and I never had to fight traffic. By this time, I had worked my way into a full-time lower management role at the YMCA and I could schedule my hours as I liked, for the most part.

A commute like the one I drove every day can be a great time to do lots of things: listen to books on tape, practice mindful breathing, listen to great music or engaging talk radio. Instead, I used that time to obsessively rake myself over the coals for every moment of my life I regretted. I began by remembering any old embarrassing moment. I felt a pang of regret in my heart or a cringe of shame on my face whenever one of my past mistakes came up in my mind for review. Invariably, I would make my way around to seeing images of Bryan tying me up or punishing me with his hand or a tool while I repeated the mantra "I can't believe I was so stupid!" to myself over and over and over. It became a ritual, and by the time I got to work each day, the car I drove felt like a prison of shame and recrimination.

Images of Bryan popped up intrusively all the time, especially during sex. *(Intrusive thoughts are a common symptom of unresolved trauma. Even with all the work I have done over the years, I still have these thoughts from time to time, and have to intentionally put up mental boundaries around them or find "tricks" to make them leave.)* I found myself comparing the sex I was having with James to the intensity of the "sessions" I had with Bryan. I tried to find ways to force the same intensity to happen with James. It never worked and often left me feeling empty and even more shameful about myself. I remember James making a comment some years into our marriage that at times he felt like there was a "ghost" in the room when we were together. In many ways, he was right on. I had no way yet to exorcise the ghost, or to let true intimacy be the source of healthy sexual intensity and contentment as well as deep connection and trust with another person.

I believe my body developed an addiction to the chemicals of traumatic response (adrenaline, norepinephrine) coupled with the chemicals that accompany arousal and orgasm (serotonin, dopamine). Whenever I was *not* in a cycle of intrigue or intensity, my body was in a state of withdrawal, just like a drug addict with no drugs. It was in that withdrawal state that I would pursue an emotional or physical affair. I literally could *not* remain completely faithful in a committed, monogamous relationship. I always justified this compulsion by telling myself "at least I'm not having sex."

My first emotional affair was with a man at work — Rick — a member at the Y who I met in the basketball gym one day while preparing to teach a class. He struck up a conversation with me, we connected a bit, and we would seek each other out for longer and longer chats while I was working. We went to lunch on a couple of occasions — as "friends," but there was plenty of flirting and intrigue going on. I knew I was playing with fire, but I could not leave him alone.

One day, Rick mentioned his fiance was going out of town, and that he could meet me outside the Y if I wanted. That scared me enough to leave him alone for a short while, but before long we were back to chatting and flirting. I never did get physical with him other than the occasional hug, but having that rush of energy in my system made me much less available for building intimacy and partnership with James, plus, I was lying to him and to myself about the "high" I experienced from having this male "friend." Emotional affairs can be just as destructive to a marriage or committed relationship as physical affairs are. I was far from done with my share of the destruction. James jumped right in with his share pretty quickly as well.

James' own addictions were a ticking time bomb. He tried a couple times to quit smoking again. He was no longer exercising regularly. His body was starting to change a lot, which drove me further away emotionally over time. He lost his job in Columbus after two years and had trouble finding another one right away, which sent him into a big depression — something he suffered with regularly, but for which I had no label or cure. Also, a genetic condition that wore down the cartilage in his knees was getting worse and he experienced variable amounts of joint pain all of the time. Though he remained abstinent from alcohol and prescription painkillers, he had never been through a true recovery process for his latent addictions or the wounds of his childhood. All he needed was a good-sized trigger for those addictions to run rampant again. The trigger came a year later.

Downwardly mobile

J AMES AND I LIVED IN COLUMBUS for a short three years. After his job loss and a long span of unemployment, he got an offer from a company in Wilmington, North Carolina. I was newly pregnant and financial stability was a top priority for both of us, so James took the job to secure a good paycheck and the health benefits we needed, even though it meant we would have to re-boot our lives once more. Being the "fresh start" girl was quickly becoming my identity since I still couldn't figure out how to remain completely faithful to my marriage. I was happy to leave behind any mistakes and tackle a new place with new possibilities and adventures. The "geographical" cure became my treatment of choice for my trauma and behavior for almost a decade before I found other tools.

We moved to Wilmington with high hopes, a pile of growing debt, and a baby girl in the oven. I needed something to do until she was born, so I hooked up some very part time work at a few nearby gyms and started volunteering at the hospital two days per week.

This still left me plenty of free time. Since I was growing bigger by the day, I wasn't exactly attracting the kind of male attention I was used to attracting, and I had all kinds of pregnancy hormones racing around inside me as well. I began to turn to compulsive masturbation to attempt to fill the emotional and spiritual hole inside that was *also* growing bigger by the day. Plus, James' health and fitness were getting increasingly bad, and I was less and less inclined to want to have sex with him either.

After living in a townhouse for a few months, we finally found a lovely modest home in a suburban neighborhood about 10-minute-drive from the beach. The neighbors were nice — one especially — a man named Joe with handsome features and dark, direct eyes. I think I melted a little the first time we met. James and I moved into the house with just enough time to unpack before I went into labor. Our daughter Blaire was born on a Sunday morning filled with sunshine and tears of joy. Though James and I were about to begin a years-long death of a marriage, we always agreed completely on one thing: how much we each loved Blaire.

Blaire kept me "happy" for almost a year. I loved being her mom. (I still do.) I loved showing her off and was grateful that I had so much babysitting experience when I was younger — I just *knew* how to take care of her and I knew what she needed. Other than the typical first-time mom challenges, like getting enough sleep and figuring out the daily eat/nap/diaper schedule, motherhood with this baby was easy.

A few weeks after Blaire was born, I got a job as a part-time program manager at a beautiful new fitness center where I loved the staff and students. I began exercising again, and was happy to find that a chronic injury that used to plague my workouts had healed. As Blaire moved through all her first year milestones, my body was beginning to bounce back, our families visited and marveled over the new arrival, and life was generally good for a while. I needed that break, because the goodness did not last long.

Trauma always wins
(until we do the work!)

S EXUAL TRAUMA IS A SLIPPERY BEAST. *Our rape culture encour-*
ages us to keep our stories hidden because they are so messy.
We would all just rather not discuss it please so "shut up and act
right" is what we trauma recipients get told, either directly or indi-
rectly. The spiritual and emotional holes that are created in the
wake of the wounds only heal from the inside out. We can attempt
to cover them up with any number of band-aids like new jobs, new
relationships, new hobbies, new homes, or relocations. Substance
(drugs, alcohol) or behavioral (sex/love, disordered eating, gam-
bling, shopping) addictions are all doomed attempts to bandage
what truly hurts. Until we stop running away from our pain or
turning outside ourselves for solutions, the wounds of trauma con-
tinue to fester in us and cause collateral damage to our friends and
loved ones. Put two trauma-shrouded people in a marriage and the

effects can be disastrous. Let's rejoin our story to find out the scope of the damage.

I became obsessed with Joe, our neighbor. When I woke up in the morning, I always went to the closet window to try to catch a glimpse of him leaving his house. I made excuses throughout each day to go to that same window and watch his comings and goings.

Since we (James, myself, and Joe) were "neighborly" anyway, I looked for ways to have him over, go borrow things, have conversations. He came to our house for Thanksgiving. He showed off his new landscaping to us. He invited us to a couple of group cookouts. If I saw he was home, I would take Blaire over and sit and chat with him while I fed her. Every time I saw him, I would get a little hit of adrenaline and my stomach would flutter. I wondered if he felt the same attraction to me that I felt for him, but I didn't have to wonder for long because he started making comments that sounded flirtatious and he never refused my bids for his company or attention.

Joe gave our whole family Christmas presents one year, and mine was an expensive bottle of perfume. My attraction for Joe was bubbling along at a level that felt mildly unsafe (I might be found out) but exceptionally thrilling (attention, favor, intrigue, secrecy) when James' dormant trauma demons were about to be triggered — but *hard*.

James' knees were getting to the point where something serious needed to be done to relieve his constant pain. He decided to repeat the surgery he had had years before to clean out shredded cartilage from the joint and hopefully reduce inflammation and improve his mobility. I thought this was a great idea and was hopeful that that would be the push he needed to get back into fitness and take better care of his body. The surgery was scheduled and we were given every impression it would be a routine procedure with a fairly quick recovery.

I drove James in for outpatient surgery and, when he got out of the OR, the surgeon reported he had found more damage than previously suspected, and had to repair a torn meniscus as well as clearing out the damaged cartilage. In the Doctor's words, "I treated him as if he were a 20-year-old, and recovery will be hard but worth it." They sent him on his way with crutches, an ice kit, and *lots* of pills. James assured me he could "handle it."

Two weeks after surgery, James was still taking several pain killers per day. I suspected something might be wrong, but I trusted the doctor when he moved James to a different "non-addictive" prescription painkiller called Tramadol. This was a synthetic drug that was supposed to give all of the pain relief of a narcotic without the dependency risks. James could not stop taking them and kept increasing the amounts he would swallow as time went on. I was with him at a work conference when he ran out of the pills with no refill available. I had never seen narcotic withdrawal before, and it is not something I ever want to see again. James turned into a sleepless, vacant, depressed, zombie for the rest of the week until we got home and he resupplied. So much for "non-addictive." I knew we were in big trouble.

James continued to take the pills. He healed up from his surgery and got off the crutches but still complained about pain, so his doctor kept prescribing the pills.

I did a little research on my own and found dozens of stories of other people suffering from dependency and withdrawal symptoms around this drug. Both the Tramadol and the Darvoset (his narcotic drug of choice) made James *seem* fine on the outside. In fact, after a while I could tell he was high whenever he *wasn't* displaying signs of depression, isolation, and irritability. However, he also needed more and more medication to be able to maintain the "normal" feelings as his addiction grew.

It was during this time that James found out his job was going to be moved overseas and that he would be downsized in a matter of weeks in November of 2003. I was 27 years old.

After the lay-off announcement, our attention shifted away from the drugs for the moment and into managing another period of unemployment. Because James had drugs this time, I didn't notice the same signs of depression that occurred with his last job loss. Thankfully, an opportunity came in before our income ran out, but it would come with a high price.

A window company in Milan, Tennessee made James an offer. Once again we were looking at a move, and this time, I was *not* excited to go. I was starting to make friends — healthy female friendships — and having a great time at my job. I had even talked to a counselor a couple of times about my wandering eyes. Even though I hadn't begun any true trauma work yet, I was becoming more comfortable with being *content*. When I filled my time with other healthy pursuits, there was less time to obsess about Joe, or any other man, for that matter. I was building self-esteem and a true support network — two things I had lacked for the last 12 years, since before I met Bryan.

I was sad and angry at the prospect of moving again and felt forced into another transition because I didn't think I could support myself and Blaire on my own, *and* I was shoving all those feelings aside, trying to be optimistic — to "make lemonade." However, I started simmering with resentment at the thought that I had no part in the decision to move simply because I was not the primary bread winner. Plus, James still got to have his drugs, which added to our financial hardships and mounting debt.

The financial stress and the addiction stress and the relocation stress finally pushed me over the edge. When James left for a few days to find a rental house in Tennessee and move some of our things, the first person I called was Joe.

I invited Joe over to the house under the pretense of having a last "neighborly" supper together. I put Blaire to bed, made sure I had talked to James one last time for the evening, as well as letting him know Joe was over for a short meal (because if I told James part of the truth, that meant I was being honest, right?)

Once I got off the phone, I was free to forget who I was and create a fantasy for an evening. The whole time Joe was at our house I kept telling myself "James gets his drugs. I get this." Joe stayed late and we ended up making out for quite a while on the couch.

Once more I tried to push away the guilt by telling myself it wasn't so bad — we didn't sleep together, but there was no sleeping that night for me. Once the high of the fantasy and the intrigue wore off, I was wide awake, my stomach was in knots, I was shaking and sweating, and I had no idea what to do. What I did next surprised even me: I went to the base of the stairs, looked up at the sky (presumably at God) and said out loud, **"If I am going to change at all, I cannot do it alone. I'm going to need some help."**

It is always a good idea to be intentional when asking out loud to "No One" for help, because one way or another, the help comes and we don't get to decide how the help feels or how the help is packaged.

I was finally asking for a way to face the pain of all my trauma, not knowing that the only way out was through. I'm glad now that I didn't know what I was in for then, because our lives were set to get a whole lot harder before they got easier. Finding rock bottom is definitely helpful (the only options are to go up or sideways), but never easy.

Step one:
We admitted we were powerless

WE MOVED TO JACKSON, Tennessee in February 2004. Blaire was a year and a half old, and I couldn't have been more grateful she was such a good little traveler. She and I made the drive over the Smokey Mountains by ourselves to meet James, who began his new job about a week before we got there. He found a rental house where we lived for about six months while we looked for a permanent place. I was always good at finding work fast, and was set to begin a part-time program coordinator position at a large new fitness center in Jackson, as well as teaching a few classes at a small YMCA fifteen miles down the road in tiny Milan, Tennessee.

I was keen to make this move into a positive step for all of us, but I was trying in vain to cover up a large pile of poo with wedding cake, as the saying goes. I missed my friends, my old job, our old home, the beautiful town of Wilmington, the beach, and the ocean.

We traded out the coast for miles and miles of cotton fields and more Baptist churches than there were gas stations. I felt as though a heavy blanket of fundamental Christianity covered the very surface of the ground as far as the eye could see. I was surprised at how hard this cultural shift was for me to digest, in addition to the regular stress of moving. I felt completely isolated — a strange woman in a strange country, and to top it off, James' drug addiction was worsening each week. He appeared functional on the outside, but I listened to him unscrew the pill bottle cap and tap the capsules into his hand each morning and I knew the truth.

I felt so helpless around James' addiction after the first few months in Tennessee that I finally sought out a psychologist — to help me figure out how to deal with *James'* problems, mind, because I thought *he was* the *problem*. I told James what I was doing and why, hoping it might change his behavior. No such luck. When I went to see the counselor, I so wanted her to tell me how to change my husband — how to get him to stop taking drugs.

Instead, she suggested I start by trying to change myself, and sent me away at the end of the hour with a list of local Al-Anon meetings. "Just go," she said. "Sit there. Those people will know how to help you."

For those readers that might be in the dark about Al-Anon, it is an international organization based on the principles of that other group, Alcoholics Anonymous. Both are anchored on the The Twelve Steps and are designed to help both the alcoholics and their friends and family recover from the disease of addiction. Al-Anon is for anyone negatively affected by the addiction of another. Today there are many other such 12-step groups that help people with specific chemical and behavioral addictions like narcotics, gambling, food, sex, porn, and codependency, among others.

So, I went one Saturday morning to a non-descript, brown, brick building near the middle of town. I wandered inside with small, defeated footsteps, unsure what to expect. Several other people trickled into a stark room with a taped-up Al-Anon sign on the door.

Someone said "Hello," and probably some other welcoming words. I don't remember. I sat. And then, as the leader began to speak, I wept. I cried and cried and tried to be quiet and then cried some more. I remember so clearly the palpable sense of utter *relief* I felt with my butt firmly in that hard, plastic, uncomfortable chair.

We started with some readings, we recited the 12 steps, a topic for discussion was announced, and newcomers were encouraged to share a little personal background. As the other attendees began to read or share on the topic of the day, I felt like I was finally *home*. I was listening to the language of *my people* — I just *knew* it. When it was my turn to talk, I said "I'm here because I want my husband to stop using drugs." No solutions were offered as I blew my nose and wiped my tears — I was told instead to "keep coming back, honey."

It took me only a few meetings to realize that this group was not supposed to help me with James, it was supposed to help me look at *myself*. I was encouraged at every meeting to "admit I was powerless over addiction and that my life had become unmanageable."

I had no trouble swallowing that statement because it was absolutely the truth. Every aspect of our lives was affected by our separate addictions (his with the chemicals, me with the infidelity) even though on the outside we looked like a run-of-the-mill family.

I was so tired of the crazy-making dance that was going on in our house — the secret, taboo cancer that was eating away at our family while all still appeared ordinary from the outside. These meetings were a place where people told the absolute truth and *survived*. Every single hour spent in a recovery room was a tiny emotional oasis in a desert of confusion and grief. I kept going back, just like everyone told me to. It was enough to have simple directions like this to follow.

By this point in time, James and I had found a permanent house in the country between Jackson and his office in Milan. Blaire was turning 2 years old that summer, and was the source of much joy and happiness as she learned new things about the world every day. Our nanny from Wilmington came to spend a good part of the summer with us, and the neighbor couple from just down the road rolled out the welcome wagon of friendship right when we moved in.

James' drug use stayed constant during this time, but I had gathered elements of support that helped me not to focus on it quite so much. Looking back, it was a relief to have these small moments of "intermission" between hardships. I'm forever grateful that there always seemed to be some kind of life "fortification" before some more walls came tumbling down.

The more Al-Anon meetings I attended, the better I felt. Al-Anon (or any of the twelve-step programs) provided a template for living that helped tremendously with my own behavioral and emotional shift. "It works if you work it" is a common slogan in "the rooms" and I can attest that it is accurate. The more I reached out to other friends in the group and focused on the ways that I was making life easier and better for *myself and my daughter,* the easier it was to see that I had choices.

I could be in a marriage and still be a sovereign person. I did not have to obsess about the addict's habits and drug use. I learned more about the disease of addiction, and knowledge was power. I could set boundaries. I could choose to feel emotions that were mine rather than waiting to see how the addict was behaving and allowing that to determine my mood. I could begin having my own dreams and start reaching for them.

After a month or two of meetings, it was recommended to me to get a sponsor — someone who had perhaps a similar story to mine, but with more experience in the program to serve as a mentor and supportive guide to life outside of meetings.

The sponsor I found was a loud and proud southern lady with a thick Jackson twang and a personality that dwarfed her small athletic frame. Deanna was a sports diva, a fashionista, a socialite, and the wealthy wife of a raging alcoholic in a steep downward spiral. I loved her and feared her in equal measure. We bonded immediately.

Deanna was the person who by her stumbling-continually-forward manner taught me about the life and the voice I wanted to have. She was big enough and brave enough to hold a strong container for me while I flailed about in search of my own healing. She brought me to every new therapeutic program she ever tried, and quite honestly, she may have saved my life. I started to take a long look at some of *my* wounds because of her, when I finally became ready.

As for me and my own destructive and damaging habits, I was distracted and despairing enough when we first moved to Tennessee that I wasn't looking to increase my own shame and depression by acting out again with some new person of interest.

I dabbled in my behaviors by emailing a few old ghosts (Joe, Rick from the Y in Columbus) and flirting online on a few occasions. After having been in Al-Anon and under Deanna's guidance, I managed to break those connections off, which felt good.

Now, because I had not yet addressed the core of my pain yet and I knew I did not want to act out any more with other people, I acted "in" instead. I began to masturbate much more often and would sometimes use pornography alongside the masturbation. This seemed to be a "safe" way to address my compulsion for sex, romance, and intrigue, but it was still just a bid for intensity and escape in the end. It took almost another year for me to let go of this "acting in" stop-gap.

Meanwhile, I think James and I still had sex now and then. I say "I think" because I remember only one specific time that we had sex after we had moved to Tennessee. In fact, as I started writing about our move to Tennessee, I had to work really hard to remember the timeline of life events in the whole year of 2005.

Living with addiction (being the active addict or the spectator) is also a form of trauma. As the partner/family of the addict, we find ourselves in hypervigilance mode — flooding our systems with stress hormones for prolonged periods of time. One symptom of trauma is "blocking out" large swaths of experience in our memories. In learning to live with an active addict, I lost almost a whole year of accurate memory.

In the fall of 2004, James entered a rehab facility for one week. He felt like he was hitting some kind of limit, I think, and couldn't deny his own drug dependency any more. No one at work knew about his drug use yet, and he wanted to keep it that way, so that's why he chose only a week of treatment — his colleagues thought he was out on vacation.

I was *so* glad to see him leave and the week without him was a wonderful break. Blaire and I went outside a lot and enjoyed the neighbors and the southern autumn beauty. It was beyond liberating to get to make all the decisions and to be unconcerned about what might be waiting for me at home when I returned.

I thought about visiting James at the treatment center, but I was so angry at him for "doing this" to our family that I stayed away. I'm sure that hurt him. It was not a very compassionate decision, perhaps, but indicative of where our marriage was ultimately headed.

James got back from rehab and was able to remain sober for a few months. After he returned, he came clean to his boss about why he had been away. All seemed well for a week or so, and then the company announced a large lay-off. I was not surprised that James' name was on the list. Here we went again.

That was the Fall that James spiraled into a depression the likes of which I have never seen before or since. He seemed eerily okay just after he lost his job, but went downhill quickly from there. He was able to receive unemployment for a number of months, so that combined with my part-time job helped pay some of our bills, but our credit card debt continued to pile up because we had not changed our lifestyle to live within our new and limited means.

He was having no luck finding another job, and when a couple of opportunities finally came up in his field, they were "not good enough" to waste time applying for. I was in utter shock at the level of denial going on in James' head about our financial situation, but remained quiet and kept going to Al-Anon meetings. I had already found out that nagging and rescuing and enabling did *nothing* to change his behavior.

Fall wore on with no offers, and the holidays were looming. Thinking some time away might be a good thing, we decided to get out of town for a while and spend Christmas with James' family in South Dakota.

Surprisingly, that Christmas was one of the nicest I can remember. We drove most of the night to get up north — I don't remember there being any serious weather on the way up. James was calm and even seemed happy. I thought he was turning some kind of corner. Blaire enjoyed her cousins and all the Christmas hullabaloo. I snuck off to the local Y for a couple of workouts and some time alone. I think we ran into a winter storm on the way home, but other than that it was a relief to be away from all the gloom in our house.

Until I found out when we got home that James had relapsed, and that the reason why it was so easy to be around him on the trip was because he was high the whole time. Ugh. Gut punch. And, a fitting end to an equally terrible year.

Who leaves who?

2005 IS A FUZZY BLUR. I struggle still today to piece together an accurate timeline of that year. I know I continued going to Al-Anon meetings. I worked longer hours, picking up personal training clients, more classes, and generally hustled any way that I could to help make ends meet. James remained unemployed and toyed with sobriety while continuing to attend his own meetings. The only bright spot, it seemed, for him during this time was the friendship he found with other members of Narcotics Anonymous.

Our financial situation began to look dire, and empowered by the principles and practices I was learning in Al-Anon, I wanted to take action to begin developing a budget and getting our debt under control. A friend had recommended the book Financial Peace, by Dave Ramsey, and this book presented the pathway I was looking for. There were baby steps to follow, which I loved. Baby steps were manageable.

I began to build an emergency savings fund by having a garage sale and purging the house of anything we no longer needed. I cut up all my credit cards, and I asked James not to put any more charges on his card either. I lined up a realtor to put our house on the market — the mortgage was killing us each month and our money hole was getting deeper.

It became a top priority to put my financial matters in order for both me and for my daughter, something I had never really done before. This was real adulting and it felt amazing. It felt amazing until a package I never ordered arrived at our doorstep — a drug refill that James charged to his credit card to the tune of $400.

I was *livid*. It finally dawned on me how much this addiction was actually costing us in terms of *dollars* — I had never asked about the cost of the drugs — James always just seemed to have them. I was absolutely *rageful* about this new information. I think I felt how James must have felt after I told him I had cheated on him back in Eau Claire. This was betrayal of the worst kind. I had begged him to help me get us out of debt by keeping true to one small promise, and *he couldn't even do this one thing.* I was done.

I moved my money immediately into a separate banking account — a separate bank entirely, actually. Doing this was another small step in claiming my power, my voice, and control over my choices. Once I signed the account papers and saw my (pitifully small) balance in an account that was solely *mine,* I knew my life could start changing in larger ways. I wanted the changes to keep coming, and fast!

At some point during 2005, James began sleeping in the guest room. I think he began to do this because he would often stay up late watching television or surfing the interwebs. I had set the boundary of asking him not to open his pill bottle in the bathroom off the master bedroom — this was a big step for me and something I learned in Al-Anon — how to stand up for myself without trying to change the addict.

By stating that it was not okay with me to wake up every morning to the shake of a pill bottle that I knew was the sound of a terrible disease, I stood up for a more positive start to each day for me. I wasn't nagging James to stop using, just drawing a line in the sand about the house we still had to share. I think it was easier for him to stay in his depression and addiction if he didn't have to see me as often, so he moved out of the bedroom. To me, this felt like he had pretty much given up on getting better or helping himself in any way. I began to wonder how much longer I could stay with him.

It's not when, it's how

E VEN THOUGH MOST OF THAT YEAR was a long, scary, confusing, painful, black journey through the soupy abyss of addiction, I can look back and see that several elements of my life were actually improving toward the wind-down of 2005.

Work was an island of normalcy for me and I was finding more ways to get paid for doing things that I loved. I had many good friends from Al-Anon who were supportive and available when rough moments and crises popped up. Blaire seemed happy and fairly oblivious to the painful undercurrents going on with myself and her father — we did our best to show her we loved her, and James tried hard, even through his depression and addiction, to be a good dad. He finally did get a job and seemed to be gaining small amounts of traction on his life.

We decided to try to hang onto the house after his paycheck resumed. Money was still pretty tight, but we were trying to manage. We were still not on the same page regarding our budget, and I struggle to remember if he was still using drugs during this time or not. However…

James could hold himself together at work, and still went to NA meetings, but his depression continued to rage at home. He was reclusive and emotionally checked out. Though he loved Blaire very much, I no longer felt comfortable leaving her with him for long periods of time.

I had come home one day after a Saturday morning out running errands to find James asleep on the couch, while she was in the same position at the kitchen counter as I left her — in her jammies watching TV, with dried-out oatmeal in front of her from several hours before. I scooped her up, hugged her close, got her dressed, and we left the house for the rest of the day. At that moment, I could only rescue her for a few hours from her father's illness. I knew I would not leave her alone with him again until I could trust he was getting the help he needed. This was the first time I was truly afraid for Blaire's safety if we stayed in the house.

I knew I was quickly reaching the end of my tolerance to stay in the marriage, but I just couldn't figure out how to go. I resolved to start piecing together a plan, no matter how small the initial steps.

I felt totally insecure writing that last part because even in the face of that concern for my daughter's welfare, we still had so much going for us. (The insecurity is my "what are you complaining about, that wasn't so bad" voice — the one that says what I experienced wasn't really so traumatic, even though the scars and emotions and nightmares are still with me today.) So many kids have suffered much more trauma at the hands of very sick parents with unresolved trauma themselves — and make no mistake, James' disease of addiction and depression nearly killed him on several occasions.

He never hit us, he never raped me, or even touched me in any way without my consent. This first visible instance of neglect of Blaire on his part was a real wake-up call for me, and going back in my mind, I can see Blaire at age 3 sitting at the counter I just described and I still shed tears of sadness and regret. Many families have painful and visible scars from the effects of unresolved trauma — Blaire and I escaped relatively unscathed.

I think about how much support I had through my recovery group as well as the fact that I had marketable skills, a college education, and all the tools I needed to make a life for my daughter and I on our own. It's really important to recognize that there are so many women today in this country and abroad who have been denied that same support, skill-base, and education only because they are women, and many times additionally because of the color of their skin. Women can't leave chronically traumatic situations without a supportive community and path toward providing for themselves and their children. Gender violence will not be over until those basic human rights are a given in every society.

Living in a small town has some advantages. Even though it can be hard to build a career in a small town, the cost of living is usually a lot lower than in a large metro area. Childcare, housing, and transportation costs can be manageable during a transition if one is careful to manage their budget.

I was able to find a one-bedroom duplex for $250 per month in Milan, Tennessee in early 2006. The daycare where I had been taking Blaire on a part-time basis offered a flexible schedule with very early drop-off, and I could bump her daycare time up incrementally as I took on more work. This way I could make sure Blaire was taken care of if I had early morning classes or clients. She also was able to come to work at the Y with me for a couple of hours per day and stay in the child watch area. I didn't have health insurance, but at least I could go to work without worrying about my daughter's care.

Once I had a line on a place to live and a few month's practice of careful cash budgeting under my belt, (Thank you, Dave Ramsey and Financial Peace!) the only step left was to leave the House of Pain, as I began referring to the house that James and I shared. I was *petrified* to go and yet I knew it was the only choice to make if Blaire and I were going to have any kind of a life or future. I wasn't so worried about what James might do to *us;* I much more concerned about what he would do to *himself* when we left.

Before I finalized my moving plans, I had gotten James to agree once more to talk to a realtor and get the house on the market. The mortgage payments were still beyond our means, and I wanted to avoid having a black mark on my credit from getting too far behind. Meanwhile, James had begun to see a doctor about his drug addiction and his inability to stay sober for long periods.

That doctor prescribed him Klonopin, which is a powerful psychotropic drug used to treat panic disorder, epileptic seizures, and alcohol and drug withdrawal. When the realtor came to the house, James was *catatonic* from the new medication. He was wandering the house and I had to lead him to the dining room table to sign the listing agreement and lead him out of the room again when it was signed. That was both a scary and repulsive moment — one of those times when I found myself wondering "How did I end up *here?*" I just wanted to disappear, and so did the realtor, I think.

As the time came closer for me to break the news to James that I was leaving, I couldn't open my mouth and say it. I remember clearly I was driving in the car when I got the "permission" I needed from beyond (or maybe from my highest, most protective and proactive self?) to take this big and imperative step.

This *voice* whispered into my right ear as I was exiting the freeway. It said "Leah. You can just *go.* You don't have to talk to him. You can wrap Blaire up and *go* to your new home. You could write a note or have a friend call him to let him know what happened. *Just go."* I breathed a sigh of relief right then and I knew I could do it. I knew everything would be okay.

The Universe has ways of cementing our intentions once we put them out there. I had left a copy of the Milan housing want-ads on the kitchen counter with a pile of work stuff. James found it one afternoon and noticed there were several ads circled. He confronted me with the ad later on and asked if Blaire and I were moving or if all of us were moving. "Blaire and I are moving out," I said. "I need a break," I said.

And so it was. He turned and walked calmly away, and that was it — for the moment. In January I plunked down the lease deposit on the tiny one-bedroom Milan duplex and planned the moving date for the beginning of February 2006. I was 29 years old.

A bittersweet new beginning

*I*T WAS SO HARD TO WRITE ABOUT THOSE LAST TWO YEARS. *Almost harder, in some respects, than writing about the sexual trauma from my youth and young adulthood. The years in the last chapters were a quagmire of guilt, sadness, crazy-making, codependency, confusion, frustration, rage, grief, and loss, mixed with growth, strength, stamina, and finally, FINALLY freedom. I fought for my freedom! I still have regular nightmares about the last two years of my first marriage. The dreams always involve James somehow being back in my life — him just appearing as if nothing ever happened, and me feeling crazy and confused and devastated at the loss of my present and healthy life, and I am voiceless. In the dreams, I scream as loud as I can inside my head "NO! This is not right — you are not supposed to be here! Where is my life — my good and right life?" And yet, I can never make the words come out. I wake up with the worst sense of despair and it takes me several minutes to shake it off and to realize that in reality, I chose the path I needed and the life I* *love — I did speak up, I used my voice and my feet and my brain and I rescued myself and my daughter from that horribly dark time.*

In the weeks leading up to my move, the air in the house was tense but resolved. I made lists of what I needed and could fit in the new place. I spoke with James about dividing our things. He seemed sad and withdrawn but put up no resistance as I prepared to go.

I asked a "handy-man" group from the church I had started attending if they could help me load up the few pieces of furniture I was taking and get them to my new place, and I lined up some help from our wonderful neighbors to keep Blaire overnight while I tried to create our new home. James waited until the last minute to say his final piece. He overdosed on Klonopin during my last week in the house and landed himself at the hospital in the intensive care unit — which said it all.

Today, I can see that the overdose was a last-resort bid to maintain the status quo made from a place of tremendous pain and illness. At the time, I was so done with *all* of it that I barely responded, thinking to myself "he can't even let me have a peaceful exit."

I have to credit Al-Anon with the strength and knowledge I needed to carry on with my move. I was able to calmly tell myself that he was where he needed to be — in the hospital — there was nothing I could do to make the situation better or worse, and that once I had myself settled, I would take Blaire to see how he was doing. His addiction no longer had power — I did.

Even though I was both angry at and worried about James, my move proceeded on schedule. Now that I had committed to providing a safe place for myself and my daughter, I guess the

Universe thought it was time that I begin working on my *own* stuff. I received a big shove from said Universe that very day.

The handymen from church showed up on a chilly February Saturday morning with several pick-up trucks and got right to work. They were *amazing,* kindhearted, hardworking, and best of all, *free.* All I had to do was point to a box or a chair or a couch, and out it went onto a waiting truck.

When they got to the bedroom, I pointed at the bed and said "that goes too." Two or three of the guys began to take it apart. All was going well until they lifted off the mattress to reveal several porn magazines and one erotic novel under the bed. I had *totally* forgotten they were still there, and I was *mortified.*

I just stood there, my face burning, wishing the floor would swallow me up whole. Once my feet would move again, I quickly piled up the Stack of Shame and shoved it back into a closet. Clearly, it was time to work on me again, but not until I had created a safe haven from which to do the work. Everyone in the room coughed and looked awkward and then we all moved on.

I spent the rest of the day moving the stuff with the handymen, and then when they were finished hauling my furniture in, I had the place All. To. Myself. This tragic little apartment was all mine. I spent the evening vacuuming up layers of dead roaches in every kitchen cabinet, bleaching every surface, scrubbing the filthy old porcelain tub, mopping the peeling linoleum, and generally being engulfed in gratitude for this one-bedroom shithole.

It was soon clean, had a sturdy lock on the door, a working heater, and even a few pictures on the wall. Blaire's room was a small tent erected in the cozy dining area, kitted out with her favorite blankets, a thick sleeping pad, and all her best stuffed animals. I couldn't wait to show her our new home. I felt so good, so... *me*. Like I had been gone for quite some time and now I could look in the mirror again and *recognize* myself.

I was dirt poor, in debt up to my eyeballs, with no long-term plan yet hashed out, and still, I was absolutely never more *sure* that all was right with the world and Blaire and I were going to be *just fine, thank you very much.*

And we *were* fine. Blaire came home with me the next day, and we settled in. I *did* take her to see her dad in the hospital. After a few days in intensive care, he was moved to a short term treatment facility in town to continue recovering.

He was still being treated for the addiction, not so much the underlying trauma. He got out of the treatment center after about two weeks and then went back to the house. Not surprisingly, he lost his job again after the whole ordeal. Now that Blaire and I were not living with him in the toxicity of the house, it was much easier to find compassion for him as well as setting and keeping firm boundaries.

I had made no decisions about whether to stay married or not yet, but I was firm about maintaining lots of alone time. I watched. I waited. I started getting busy on my own healing process. Though James and I would go through months of back-and-forth, still trying to see if there was a marriage to be saved, I think I was making little choices to leave with each passing day.

Meeting me

T HE SEVEN MONTHS BLAIRE AND I SPENT IN OUR NEW PLACE were precious and crystalline in my memory. We lived a very simple existence then. I worked, she went to daycare, and came with me to a lot of meetings with a stack of books and toys in her "busy" bag. I definitely got the kid I needed, because she was pretty good at sitting and playing quietly during all those life-saving hours I spent in The Rooms.

Sundays, I used to clip coupons and read the paper — my one weekly luxury. Blaire would often nap next to me on the couch and I felt so *safe* that I sometimes fell asleep beside her. A couple times a month we would get coupons in the mail for Sonic or Wendy's and we would walk to get a cheap dinner out with a few bucks of "fun" money I set aside in one of my budgeting envelopes. The library (also within walking distance) was our chief source of entertainment — I think we borrowed every video they had!

Though being broke was hard, I believe the lack of money contributed to my recovery. When there was nothing to spend, I had no choice but to sit with, observe, confront, and finally, *embrace* myself. I began to like small parts of me. I began to feel good about finally *becoming* an adult, instead of *pretending* to be one.

I got really good at making and keeping budgets! I was starting to take tiny bites out of my debt (which totaled over $16,000 at its highest) and I found more ways to bring in money doing the things I loved.

I wrote some continuing education material for other fitness instructors and trainers, and took my show on the road that summer of 2006. Blaire got to go up north to my parents' house for a few weeks, and I financed the trip by conducting seminars all the way home at several small and large gyms along the way. It was fun and empowering to feel so in charge of my own present moment and to start creating a life I liked.

The quiet time I enjoyed at our place at night was a sanctuary — it was holy, almost. I could feel anything or nothing. I didn't have to worry about anyone but myself after Blaire was in bed. I could *breathe.* I slept well and sound in that place as every day I learned more about my own strength, fortitude, and perseverance, and *power.*

I had always thought that my role in life was to please older men who would then take care of me. For as long as I could remember, I was only able to see myself through the (sexual) approval of someone else, whether it was my father, boys from school, Daniel, Bryan, Jack, James, or all those men with whom I had affairs. In the space between men I was learning that the only approval that really mattered was my *own*.

Even as I was growing up so much in my practical, providing-for-our-needs life, I still had a ton of work to do on my sexuality. I had begun seeing a therapist who suggested I try to stop masturbating. I had given her all the background on my acting out and acting in behavior, and she said that a break from all sex would be a healthy choice.

I was not a fan of this news. I was really scared of the word "celibacy." I thought that word was pretty much reserved for monks, nuns, or people who just couldn't get a date on a Saturday night. Not for me, a young and vibrant woman who thrived on sexual attention, and barring that, romance and fantasy.

I had made some progress. I was still married and doing a good job setting boundaries with my behavior around other men. Some of those boundaries included not baring my midriff (plenty of fitness people thrive on wearing skimpy workout clothes — I was one of them), keeping doors and windows open when training male clients or in meetings with men, and recognizing when I was using flirting behavior with men — I did not want to be sending mixed messages of any kind.

This was a steep learning curve and I stumbled often to find a balance between being warm and inviting to all people (a function of my job) and also being tuned into when I or someone else was crossing a "line" of flirtation or being too familiar too fast.

It was really important to give myself a ton of grace during this process and to share my struggles in meetings and with my sponsor and therapist. As long as I was not being secretive, I could keep a healthy light on my experimentation, and it was okay to make mistakes.

I feel compelled here to clarify a couple of things: 1. Any woman can choose to wear or not wear whatever she likes and she shouldn't have to worry it will be assumed she is "asking" for sex, attention, whistles, cat-calls, whatever. All bodies are sacred, beautiful, and worthy of love, care, and respect no matter what they look like or how they are dressed. 2. For me, in our (rape) culture and especially in the industry in which I chose to work (fitness), the way I dressed seemed to invite the kind of attention I was becoming aware was not productive or healthy for me, so I changed how I dressed.

This is rape culture. There are still times when I would love to bare more of my body and feel totally okay about it because of temperature, mood, comfort, expression, feeding a baby, or simply wanting to enjoy the same freedom as men who can go topless any old time they want. I censor myself because of what judgements or assumptions I may face as a woman doing these things — I'm being too sexual, trying too hard for my age, or I'm attention-seeking. Gender-based cultural clothing restrictions, whether implied or enforced, are a significant and changeable sign of rape culture.

I was beginning to notice when I held up my own boundaries that I attracted different sorts of people into my life. For example, I once had a male client who I enjoyed working with. This was a novelty because most of my clients were either elderly or female or both. I found him somewhat attractive (which concerned me at first — would I be able to handle it?), and I believe he thought the same of me. However, I maintained my personal limits with him, continued to stay current with my therapist and sponsor, and after a time, I began to find points of real connection with him that were within a professional scope and had nothing at all to do with flirting or sexual intrigue.

We got real work done in every session, and a little at a time I found out some more about his job, or family, or interests, but at a pace that felt natural and ordinary… things you would expect to find out about someone who came in for a weekly appointment.

When I finally left my role at that gym, he gave me a card with some lovely words of praise for my ability, knowledge, and professionalism over the course of our working relationship. *that* kind of praise was truly validating and all I had to do to earn it was to be myself. And, I was not trying to get him to validate me in any way, I just wanted to do my job and do it well. The praise came of its own accord. What a concept.

So, back to the solo sex. With all the other behavior change I was trying, I was finding sex with myself to be less-than-satisfying anyway. When I did engage, I worried that it was unhealthy or a lie or just bad, which took all the fun out of it. I suppose this was a good thing then, because I was able to stop completely for eighteen months

I think my body just needed a sexuality time-out. The "space" that the lack of any kind of sex was giving me was a healing space, a reflective space, a space for me to figure out what was *true* about my own sexuality, rather than simply making someone *else's* sexuality work in order to gain their favor and approval.

I still was not sure what was going on with James and me long-term, so for now a bit of sexual limbo seemed to be right where I was supposed to hang out. Fine then. I ended up "hanging out" for a whole year and a half in one-day-at-a-time celibacy (there is that scary word again). I didn't die.

Trending up

O NCE I GOT A LITTLE MORE PRACTICE BEING SMART with what I now *had, I* began to give myself permission to want more. I wanted things like a nicer apartment, to be debt-free, a better job with real benefits, health insurance, places to have different kinds of *fun*, a town that gave more opportunity for growth.

I was *hungry,* after being confined to the small cave of addiction and depression, for *all* life had to offer. Even though I was still filled with gratitude for where I was and what I had, I was bursting at the seams to try out more of my brand new *life!* Never being one to sit still and rest on my laurels for very long, I got off my butt and started looking around for *all of the things* — starting with a new job.

I began to search out a full-time management position with the YMCA. It took about two months of networking and interviewing, and then I landed a position as the Fitness Director in a brand new branch opening in Bellevue, Tennessee, which is a western-edge suburb of Nashville.

News of the opening landed in my lap on the last day for applications, and the process was fast-tracked as the facility was opening in just a few weeks. Serendipitously, I was given an offer and twenty-four hours to accept. I was still trying to figure out where I was with the marriage, but here was an opportunity that appeared tailor-made for Blaire and I. I leapt at the chance for a new life on healthier terms. This time, I was not running *away* from pain and destructive behavior, I was running *toward* a new destiny — a new land for continued discovery and healing and growth. All felt right — I signed on the dotted line.

Providence and several Al-Anon friends aided my search for a place to live, and I found a quaint and cozy garage-apartment at the end of a beautiful wooded street on the very outskirts of town.

From where I was coming from, it may as well have been a mansion in paradise. It was a no-brainer to sign the lease. I was beyond happy and expansive with grace.

Oh, and the mortgage that was killing me financially? Just as I was preparing to leave for Nashville, a short-sale offer came through, and after several weeks of bank paperwork and nail-biting, I was free of the House of Pain about a month after I moved away. Praise the Universe and all its benevolence!

Moving to Nashville meant leaving James behind for the time being. About this I felt guilty and empowered all at the same time, which is a crazy-making place to be. I did not want to pull Blaire away from her dad, but I knew we could not thrive with him either, and I was getting serious about what marriage meant to *me*. I had set some boundaries around myself that affected James, but were really more about me and what I wanted in a true partner. The stronger I felt about those boundaries, the more disgusted I got with James.

I asked that before James and I talked about getting back together that he stop smoking, stay sober from drugs, and find and keep a job that supported him and half of Blaire's expenses. This may have been a lot to ask of a newly recovering addict, but for the first time I was no longer willing to compromise my own needs or limits so someone else could feel comfortable in their dysfunction. I still had plenty of my own healing to work through, for Pete's sake, and did not need to worry about codependency with another adult!

Also, being still legally married when I moved effectively took any sexual acting out off the table for me… I felt good about the sexual sobriety I had worked so hard for within the marriage, and that stability was paramount to my continued healing during the stress of the relocation, no matter how excited I was to be going away.

Being "single" was just not something I was ready for — yet. And, I probably need to call myself out here. Staying in a de facto marriage meant that at least for a while, I did not have to feel the failure of the relationship, and I didn't have to be the "bad guy" who split up the family with a small child in the mix. I was scared, in all honesty, of the bigness of that decision and I just didn't want to be the one to make it. Also, I was on the very cusp of diving into the work of attending to my original trauma wounds in a very unexpected way, just before starting over in Nashville.

Trauma camp

I WAS STILL VERY MUCH INVOLVED IN AL-ANON and intended to find a new home group in Nashville as soon as I got there. I was also still seeing a therapist, and intended to continue meeting with one in the new city as well.

My sponsor Deanna had been so supportive of my process and I had also been watching her confront her own sex and love addiction and had sometimes accompanied her to a 12-step group called SLAA, Sex and Love Addicts Anonymous. Little by little I was preparing to come to terms with my trauma, but the Universe was doing all the planning and orchestrating to bring me where I needed to be, not me. I had no idea what I was about to do, I just kept saying "yes" when an opportunities came up.

Deanna had invited me to go to a weekend intensive therapy group put on by the Experiential Healing Center of Memphis Tennessee. It was at a summer camp just outside Mount Olive, Mississippi.

The image I see when thinking about this weekend is toothpaste being squeezed out of a tube — there is no putting the toothpaste back inside the tube once it is out. I was the tube, my trauma was the toothpaste, and all that goop was about to be splattered over the walls, ceilings, and floors.

Deanna and I arrived at Trauma Camp on a warm Friday morning, and I had no idea what to expect. We checked in, put our stuff into our bunks, and then were separated out into small groups to work with one of 4 or 5 Experiential Therapists.

The first day was to be spent in these smaller groups, and the following day would be spent all together as a large group with all of the staff. My therapist was a man named Sam. With his big belly, Hawaiian shirt, beard, glasses, and happy squinty eyes, he was a cross between the Buddha and Santa Claus, with a heavy dose of tie-dye hippy thrown in for good measure. There were about eight of us in his group, both men and women, many of us there for the first time.

Sam began by explaining what the experiential model of therapy is: A role-playing exercise where one person selects others from the group to serve as players in a "sculpt" of a past traumatic experience. The "main character" might put herself in the sculpt or not, but the point is to recreate the experience so the feelings can be felt and worked through, often with the opportunity to say was might have been left unsaid in the actual event, or to act in such ways that the initial trauma response (fight, flight, or freeze) may have prevented in the moment the trauma occurred.

For example, a survivor of domestic abuse might choose a group member to play her abusive spouse. She can then have the chance to rage at him, "hit" him (figuratively, with a number of safe props), or leave him. Or, she could choose another group member to play herself in the same situation, and she can "rescue" herself from that same traumatic experience.

Re-enacting the trauma scenario gives the survivor a sense of control over the situation that she did not have while it was actually happening. Also, reliving the experience in a controlled setting like these groups allows the survivor to experience real feelings about what happened and work through a normal grief and loss process which can provide a path to closure and healing.

When the feelings are processed, the traumatic memory gets properly "filed" in the brain and the survivor can experience relief from secondary trauma symptoms like addictive behavior, flashbacks, traumatic repetition, nightmares, depression, or anxiety, to name a few. While this type of therapy is not a one-time miracle cure for the symptoms of unresolved trauma, over time it can be a major part of the solution for many trauma survivors.

To break the ice in our small group, Sam started by having us pretend to ride motorcycles, dance around in crazy ways, stretch and bend, and generally loosen up. Then, members of the group began to take turns "sculpting" the events on which they wanted to work.

Though I don't remember anyone's work specifically, I remember being chosen to play a mom, a sister, or an auntie role for several different group members. I watched my fellow group members rage, cry, hit pillows with baseball bats, emerge from piles of pillows as if fighting to be reborn, hug and receive affirmation or deliver forgiveness. I was a willing participant in the sculpts of others that first day, and a bit unsure of what I wanted to work on when it was my turn.

The following day, all of the small groups gathered together to watch the "star" of the weekend recreate her whole life in a sculpt — this was a very work-intensive process that took many months to put together.

As we watched the sculpt unfold through the morning and afternoon, we were encouraged to journal, laugh, cry, shout, rage or emote in other ways as we found pieces of the sculpt that were relevant for us as this person was doing the bulk of her healing work.

It was moving to watch her process and to share in the burdens, joys, addictions, shame, and relationships she and her "cast" were acting out. Still, I hadn't really cracked open yet myself, and I thought maybe that's all there was — a few tools to take with me and the honor of watching someone else be vulnerable and brave on a therapeutic stage. We had one more day to go.

The next morning we were back in our small group with Sam, the Hippie-Buddah-Santa therapist. I remember we were sitting on the floor in a loose circle. He was passing around a toy baseball bat — sturdy, but light, with a solid core and a spongy covering, red and black in color — and talking about anger. Even as I write out the memory, I can feel butterflies in my stomach — I was sure that I did *not* want to hold the bat.

The bat made its way toward me anyway, and I went into a bit of a trance when it finally sat in my hands. I kept staring at it, not knowing how to feel. Sam must have noticed that my face or demeanor changed, because he asked me if I wanted to hit anything. I said "yes."

A chair with a large red, nylon covered pillow was prepared. Other group members had hit it over the weekend and it made a loud "crack" every time the bat landed. The sound startled me each time — I was a afraid of the anger it provoked. It was never okay for me to be *angry* in my trauma — only accommodating, acquiescing, being a subservient sexual plaything, a submissive and powerless player in a drama someone else had scripted, or a shameful, deceptive daughter who betrayed her family. My rage was bubbling over as I tightened my grip on the bat and the pillow was secured by my fellow group members.

When everything was ready and Sam said "*Go,*" the scream from my throat was *deafening* to my own ears, and the *fury* I rained down on the pillow was *inexhaustible*.

Over and over, I landed blow after blow on the pillow — "Whack, slam, crash, whack, slam, crash!" There began a rhythm to my swings, and I screamed until my throat was raw, and my group members looked on — some cried, some encouraged me, some were watchful and quiet, maybe thinking about who or what *they* wanted to hit when their turn came.

I kept going — wailing and screaming until I was sweaty and my arms were *done* and my mouth was dry. I took a break to breathe. I wilted, the bat limp in my worn-out hand.

I didn't know what to do next. Everyone came around me — they surrounded me in support and encouragement! They assured me that what I did was *awesome and absolutely needed to come out*, and what my piece of work had brought up for them.

I no longer had to bottle up my anger, but I had only scratched the surface, it turned out. A calming song was played to disperse some of the intense energy I had unleashed, and eventually another person took their turn with the bat.

In these several explosive minutes, a new space had opened up in me. I felt different — powerful and spent all at the same time, and completely surrendered to the process at work inside me. I wanted more of this cleansing, this lightness, this *sublimation* — *this* is what I had been searching for in all the men, the porn, the shame, and later in the Al-Anon meetings and rote behavior change, to no avail.

This space was the stuff of God. The stuff of Me. The space where God and I could begin to create something new together, and *that,* dear reader, was *grace.*

Later on that day, I did another piece of work. During the earlier bat exercise, my rage was directed all at Bryan — for the shame, humiliation, manipulation, brainwashing, and repeated rape he delivered over the course of our involvement together. In this next piece of work, my parents, specifically my mother, was on the receiving end of the anger.

Despite what happened in our house when I was a teenager, my mother had always been pretty close to me. Though she loved my sister and I equally, she was a different mother to each of us — probably due to the fact that she had birthed us so far apart in age. She was a different person when she had my sister at age 25, as the wife of an alcoholic, then a single mother struggling through college, than with me at age 36, in a secure marriage and with ten more years of life experience. She often called me the "child of her heart" and had no filter around sharing stories of her life with me. I learned as a young teenager about her school-age crushes and boyfriends, and she told me about an affair she had had while her first marriage was ending. She gave me some of her teenage journals replete with details about this boy or that boy, whom she had kissed and for how long, how she snuck out of the house or the resort, etc.

It felt kind of yucky to know those things about her then, but I didn't want to disappoint her by not reading them, so whatever, I looked over the material. There was also that one time that she had a psychic reading from a woman in Florida who mentioned to my mother that she was sure that my mom and I were twins in a past life. My mom seemed to attach herself to this revelation, and she repeated it to me often in my twenties. It was very awkward and made me feel slimy and like I wanted to take a long shower. I imagine today that all of that behavior probably came from some kind of unresolved pain and the corresponding need for validation, but that did not make it easier to be on the receiving end of the smothering blanket of our enmeshed mother-daughter bond.

Back to Trauma Camp and my next piece of work. It was chaotic — a jumble of emotions. I cannot remember what the lead-up was in the group, or how I came to my next turn in the spotlight, or what I told the group about my mom, if anything.

I only remember feeling smothered and suffocated by my mother's energy all of a sudden in that room — so much so that the red pillow was again brought out for me — this time, to push against — literally pushing my mother's energy off of me so I could breathe.

Several group members lined up holding the red pillow and couple of other cushions. Sam had me walk up to the "pillow wall" and start pushing. As soon as I started, I could not stop. I pushed and pushed and the pillow wall moved back. I pushed and screamed and the pillow wall moved more. At one point, I looked up and there were — *no bullshit* — four *very* burly men holding the pillows while I steadily moved all of the guys back toward the far wall of the room!

We had to stop because all four of them were on the wall and could not hold me back anymore. I fell into a tired and hoarse heap on the floor, and again received validation and encouragement from the group while a calming song played in the background to help us all come down from the intense work.

More space inside me opened up then, just like earlier in the day. A crack of light shone into the space, and I could finally see that maybe there was a way to tunnel out of the cave of pain that had been plaguing my life for over a decade. This was a first foray into the depths of grief and loss that had remained buried under *years* of shame, codependency, and addictive behavior.

I had faced down two powerful demons and *survived*. The rage did not kill me, it strengthened my resolve to keep going. I didn't know how long the recovery road would be, but armed with my own voice and the support of other survivors, I knew I was ready for the mountains ahead.

When trauma is not processed in a healthy way with plenty of guidance from experienced helpers, those memory "files" remain scattered on the floor of the brain, and we keep tripping over them whenever triggers arise. We are forced to continue to relive the trauma until we find our unique healing path that helps us to file the memories away as part of our overall story. With help and treatment, we can begin to see that trauma has a beginning and an end — we are no longer prisoners of the middle.

Onward, to Music City!

J UST A COUPLE OF WEEKS AFTER TRAUMA CAMP, I packed up the moving truck *again* and headed off into the land where (country music) dreams come true!

The drive from Jackson to Nashville was a short three hours, but I felt like I was moving yet again to another country. As I drove, the landscape metamorphosed from cotton fields out beyond the horizon to rolling rises, rivers, trees, and finally large jagged rocks and even cliffs.

The land reflected my insides as well — leaving behind a flat, growth-less life where depression and baseline gloom had loomed for so long, to embracing a life of color, contour, and vibrancy, if not ease and comfort. I had no illusions about the challenges of single motherhood or starting over yet again. The happy part for me was that I was the one in charge, and ooooooooh, that felt *so* good!

Blaire handled the move okay, I think. She had the benefit of being young (4 years old) and resilient, plus her father was adamant about staying an important part of her life, and she had at least somewhat adjusted already to not living with him all the time. She liked our new home where she had a larger room all her own, and wildlife that sometimes traipsed across our back yard.

My sponsor Deanna called me out on trying to do for Blaire what I had once done for myself, which was to gloss right over any feelings of loss around leaving. I had been telling Blaire that our move would be exciting and fun, emphasizing that mommy's new work would have a pool with a waterslide she could use all the time! No room for any moping or sadness with all this fun to be had! I had to take a step back and honor her space too, which was not always easy.

Even though she transitioned fairly well overall, Blaire had several hiccups figuring her way into new friendships or wanting to become too close too soon to some of my male colleagues at work she had occasion to see on the regular. I will never know what was really going on in her little head and heart during that time... she says she doesn't remember very much of those early days.

My new job was both good and bad. I made friends quickly with several other managers and the building itself was state-of-the-art. The members were fun to get to know and our fitness classes and programming started to take off right as we opened the doors.

However, I had so much to figure out — the center itself was enormous already and the membership was exploding beyond anyone's expectations. I had a lot of responsibility and was a bit out of my leadership depth. Also, I was still searching for recognition and validation — those habits die hard — and now that I was not on the hunt for it in relationships, I shifted the search into the framework of my job.

I ended up taking on way too many projects early on to try to garner attention, and suffered some nasty falls along the way. I found my feet finally, but not until after a few painfully humbling dress-downs by my superiors.

Looking back, it is a miracle I kept my job there for as long as I did. Today I am really grateful for all leaders who see and believe in the potential of people like me — single parents trying to make a go of our lives and support our kids, stumbling forward a few steps and then a backward drop until we get it right.

My personal life in the new place was pretty boring for a couple of years — exactly as it should have been. Happily, Sam the Hippie-Santa-Buddha, had an office a couple of miles from my home, so he became my new regular therapist, *and* he had a sliding fee scale I could afford.

I continued my work with him, I got involved in a church and met a few people who invited me to hang out for brunch and stuff, and I also found two 12-step meetings — a convenient Al-Anon chapter (well, three of them, actually) as well as a Sexaholics Anonymous group.

One group was to help me deal with James (we were still married, after all, and had not decided what to do next) and the other was to help me deal with me and my addictive sex/love behaviors.

Even though I had begun some serious trauma work and was on a good path, changing long-ingrained compulsive activity is an everyday challenge. I'm not sure what I would have done had it not been for these two life-saving groups in a new place full of temptations.

Getting used to being "just me" was a daily struggle. I craved love and intrigue and romance all of the time, especially because everything was new and I was trying to build stability — it was hard to remain grounded in the face of so much possibility.

I looked around with jealousy — sometimes at a maddening level — at people I knew who seemed to have what I wanted: A handsome, wealthy, man who was crazy about me, a comfortable lifestyle, a two-parent team who truly had it together. It was painful to think I might never have that. I had no idea how to go about getting it and I could see this lifetime of loneliness stretching out beyond the horizon.

I have always had a flare for the dramatic. It was very difficult for me to take a longer practical view, so I felt *all* of the things in every extreme, as if my life were over in one minute or I was on the top of a mountain of joy and excitement the next. There was no middle of the road at all. I had to practice living with "medium" and it sucked most of the time.

And yet there were moments during that first year that were filled with such grace for Blaire and I. I remember taking Blaire to the opening of a fancy concert hall in the heart of the city. It was a beautiful autumn afternoon, and Blaire had chosen to wear a set of fairy wings over her little jacket.

We walked around downtown, sampled food and listened to music at the event. She was really enjoying it, and I watched with pride and gratitude as everyone who passed her on the street gave her a wistful heartfelt smile, a wave, a wink. I thought about the instant of joy she brought to others as she paraded her little fairy self up and down the sidewalk, holding onto my hand. Her innocence was pure and her beauty was infectious. And all she had to do to radiate that out into the world was be herself.

Blaire and I spent our first six months both conquering the town and holing up in our nest in the woods. There were some ups and downs as we adjusted. One such roller coaster was "divorcing" myself from my parents.

After Trauma Camp, I found myself struggling during routine phone calls with my mom and dad. It got so bad that whenever my mom called me I felt nauseated, almost to the point of vomiting.

I didn't know how to fix it and my sponsor said it was probably a result of all the anger I unleashed from the recent experiential therapy. Deanna supported me in writing to ask my parents for an undetermined period of "no contact," meaning, I had to speak up for the space I needed, even though I didn't know what to do during that time.

Writing that letter was terrifying — there was a big understood family contract in place about not "hurting Mom," and that had been our governing mode of operation for years. I had no idea what would become of our relationship in the end, but learning to ask for what I needed was an essential part of my ongoing recovery. This was adulting at a profound level.

The request *did* hurt my parents tremendously, but that did not change how much I needed space and time to work through what I was feeling. After a number of months, I was able to begin speaking to them again — to carefully rebuild some kind of connection based less on codependency and so much more on my fledgling ability to approach them as a true grown-up who was still their daughter, but did not *need* them for validation or to be my *parents* any more.

The struggle to change is real

W HILE TRYING TO BUILD A LIFE BETWEEN THE EXTREMES, there were all sorts of triggers lurking everywhere to invite me to revert to old patterns. Even in Al-Anon meetings there were plenty of men who fit my default pattern: much older than me, affluent, and intense. One such man was named Tom.

I met Tom at the very first Nashville Al-Anon meeting I attended. In a room chock-full of interesting people, I picked him out with one glance. He was tall, attractive, a good speaker during the meeting, open about his feelings during his sharing time, and of course, possessed of a direct ice-blue gaze that made my stomach flip-flop.

Now, I knew *any* man was a no-no for the moment, but looking back, the addict inside me started laying the groundwork for a big relapse that very afternoon. When people were milling around after the meeting, Tom came over to say "hello" and welcome me as a newcomer to the meeting. Our exchange was brief, but memorable for me. I found out he had a motorcycle. I already had my own helmet. I was in big trouble.

I saw Tom here and there at meetings and sometimes at after-meeting meals with smaller groups. Later that first fall in Nashville, he and I ended up at the same "orphan" Thanksgiving party hosted by another Al-Anon member.

Tom and I exchanged some more conversation, and I found out that like me, he was just exiting his marriage and that his life was as much of an emotional mess as mine. We chatted about normal things like jobs and interests and other polite dinner talk. We left it at that, for the time being.

Meanwhile, I was getting down and dirty with the 12 steps in my SA meetings. I had found a sponsor in that group — Penelope. She was lovely, accepting, friendly, and supportive. She got me started journaling my way through each step without shame or judgement, and I made a lot of headway sorting through some of the yucky sexual history I had amassed to that point. I could see and own much of my addictive sexual behavior, as well as starting to recognize that the beginning of that behavior occurred right after I was first molested by Bryan. Trauma just keeps right on giving.

It is one thing to attend 12 step meetings and another thing entirely to "work" each step. That is where the real recovery happens. When we meditate, journal, and dialog on each step, we start to live them out in a way that is productive and transformational. This practice is not a guarantee against further acting out or trauma repetition (as I would prove in a couple of years), but it goes a long way toward re-shaping a life of addictive behavior. The process works best when entered into with a trusted sponsor who has done the work herself.

Even if relapse occurs, once we have walked the steps, we cannot ever engage in the same behavior again without knowing what we know, and, the steps remain faithful, present, ready, and accepting of us whenever we are ready to return to them again. The following are paraphrased from the AA and Al-Anon Big Books. Each 12 step group has the 12 steps and a primer for working them within the recovery context of the respective group, be it sex, drugs, food, gambling, or other.

I breezed right through steps 1, 2, and 3: We admitted we were powerless over sex and love and that our lives had become unmanageable. (So true, though I was starting to learn how to manage *without* compulsive masturbation, porn, sex, love, romance, and intrigue.) We came to believe that a power greater than ourselves could restore us to sanity. (I had no trouble believing in God, or the Universe, the Source, the Collective. Those are some of the names I use — I trust it — She/He/It has never let me down).

And, lastly, We made a decision to turn our will and our lives over to the care of the God of our understanding. (Yep, there was so much goodness that happened when I was able to let go and stop trying to fix and control everything myself — I still got in my own way a lot, but I could now make a decision to surrender my actions to my higher power much of the time.)

Step 4 was grueling: Made a list of all our defects. (The shortest step, but the longest process. A complete documentation of my sexual history — the good, the bad and the ugly. "Defects" is a broad term, I took it to mean everything for which I still held shame — the sorting process of right/wrong would come in the next step.)

Step 5, Survivable with a good sponsor: Admitted to God, to ourselves and to another human being the exact nature of our wrongs. (This is a cataloging of sorts, with a witness, for where we were in the wrong in our actions and need to take responsibility, and also where we were *not* in the wrong — like rape, molestation, rape cultural norms, other trauma.

Most of the time a sponsor can help us to sort out when we are being too hard on ourselves and also when we need to step up to the plate. For me, most of what happened before age 21 was not my choice, but most of everything after that age had shades of personal choice and were things that I felt sorry about, for hurting someone else with my choices.)

Step 6, Became entirely ready for God to remove these defects of character. (Again, with the language. The steps have been around for awhile, so one could substitute "pain," "shame," "resentment", etc for "defects." And, yes, I was pretty ready for the pain and shame around my trauma to go away. My acting out behavior was a harder thing to be ready to have expunged from my personal record, as time would bear out, but still, progress was made here.)

Step 7, Humbly asked God to remove our shortcomings. (Right, so basically living this out might mean that we meditate and slow down before acting on many decisions in our lives so that our often traumatic triggers do not get the best of us over and over again.)

Step 8, Made a list of all persons we had harmed and became willing to make amends to them all. (For me, this meant clear discernment of where my actions had truly hurt someone, versus when I did *not* have to take on that responsibility. For example, Bryan sent me a small package of some items I had left at his house a few weeks after we broke up, with a note saying how much I had hurt him. I was not about to apologize in a million years for leaving him and attempting to take my life back after the manipulation and mind fuck I had endured for six years of knowing him.)

Step 9, Made direct amends to such people whenever possible, except when to do so would cause harm. (I said I was sorry to the people I still knew, and for the rest I vowed not to hurt someone in the same fashion ever again. This is called a living amends — when our apology is not direct, but rather in the form adopting a different way to live.)

Step 10, 11, and 12 are all about continuing to take personal inventory, admitting when we are wrong as soon as we make a mistake, improving our contact with our Higher Power, and trying to practice all the 12-step principles every day. These are the steps we addicts keep on our top plates daily if we are intentional about creating a transformed life.

It was during the height of my step work when Tom crossed my radar again. We seemed to be getting thrown together more often in the recovery community, and I struggle today to remember how much he or I or fate initiated our contact.

In September of 2007, we went on a motorcycle ride together. It was lovely — exhilarating to be back on a motorcycle again. We talked about Al-Anon stuff, all kinds of feelings, spirituality, hopes and dreams, plus when we got to a very high bridge on the road, we stopped to look at the view, and he kissed me as some rain was beginning to roll in. (I mean, come on, can we not almost hear the music swelling in the background...?)

I could have allowed this date to hook me right back into my same pre-recovery patterns. The difference between a date like this in recovery versus a date in non-recovery is that I told everything to my sponsor afterward. She suggested that I may not yet be ready for dating, and that I should let Tom know the specific type of recovery I was doing.

Oof. I did *not* want to do this, but my progress was too important to let it all go so I trusted Penelope and made a plan to talk soon with Tom. When he called up the next day to ask me on another date, I took a deep breath and came clean about my general sex/love addiction behavior, as well as telling him I would not be able to keep seeing him at that time. He was a little puzzled, but gracious, and we hung up as friends.

I managed to hold it together during the phone call, but then afterward I broke down and *lost it*. I sobbed and sobbed and felt like my insides were ripping to shreds. Why such a dramatic response? Because Tom was my drug of choice, and my inner two-year-old who really, *really* wanted all that "candy" was being told "Nope! Too much sugar today, you can't have it," by the adult me who was trying very hard to remain in the emotional and behavioral driver's seat.

Penelope also cautioned me that it might be a good idea to take a time-out from Al-Anon meetings where I knew I would see Tom. I was not excited about this suggestion, but did manage to get some space for myself and cool off some of those intense infatuation feelings. After a few weeks, I felt better and more committed to my process again.

I shared this story because no one in recovery is perfect. Everyone "screws up" on their healing paths and trauma recipients are no exception. I think the important take-away from the 12 steps is that though this pathway toward healing is a continuous spiral constantly bringing us back around to more layers we have yet to confront, it *can* bring about new behavior, perspective, presence, and progress. Once we stop denying our past, our present, and our pain, we can never feel quite the same way about using our old and outmoded coping strategies of addiction and other destructive actions.

Make no mistake, trauma is real, can have debilitating and long-lasting effects, is unpredictable, and well, traumatic. However, being a survivor of trauma is not a blank check for staying sick and behaving badly. There is still plenty of responsibility for the survivor to own up to mistakes and to try to be a decent and functioning human being.

There is also a responsibility to *ourselves* to find pathways through the shadows of trauma. Shame, hatred, depression, nightmares and all the rest are today very *treatable* with the right help. Forgiveness is possible whether justice for the abuser is served through the courts or not, though using our voices to fight for that justice can be part of our overall healing process. 12-step work is one way to begin to free ourselves from the prison of unresolved trauma, one day at a time.

Discovering authentic sexuality

B Y THE TIME I HAD GOTTEN THROUGH ALL THE STEPS with my sponsor Penelope, some months had gone by. After a last-ditch attempt at some marriage counseling several months earlier, James and I were at a stalemate, and finally decided to cut each other loose in the fall of 2007. Papers were drawn up and the filing process started. Since we were both completely broke and still each in our own pile of debt, there were no assets to split. We saw mostly eye to eye on the custody issue (I would have primary custody of Blaire, with generous visitation from her dad) and just had to wait out the state-mandated time period, and then our divorce could be finalized.

A few months after that setback with Tom, I was really beginning to want to explore dating again (or something, for crying out loud!) I had remained completely celibate for a year and a half by this point and had focused most of my free time on recovery work. I was attending 3 or 4 meetings per week in either Al-Anon or SA,

I went to an intensive experiential therapy program (more trauma camp) at a treatment center called Onsite just outside of Nashville and had peeled back several more layers of trauma gunk, I had gotten out to be social and have fun while continuing to work on boundaries with men and friendships with women, and I felt like it was time to start dusting off the old sexuality again (gulp!)

I had learned that such big decisions in the addict world are best tackled with help, so I talked to one of the sexual addiction specialists from my first Trauma Camp about where to begin. She suggested that figuring out sex with myself would be good knowledge to have before trying to stumble through sex with another person. We talked about not using porn or fantasy to escape, rather staying in my body and creating an experience that felt *intimate*. Hmmmmmm. Intimacy with myself — what did that even mean?

Well. Here is what it meant to me. After a couple of days of wanting to dive in, but feeling scared that I would mess it up, I finally set aside some time. Yes, I planned a romantic date with myself, in the interest of being *intentional... present.*

Blaire was out of the house for the night visiting her father, and the timing just felt right. I ate a nice dinner. I played music. I lit candles and played some trancy, groovy music. I did a little yoga to loosen up, and then, I took off my clothes.

I moved my hands all over my skin slowly, trying to savor the experience. I giggled a bit at myself that I was so nervous — I wanted to do right by me and value myself in a way no one else ever had before. I observed my own arousal for several minutes — honoring what was going on as a natural, wonderful, human response to touch and tenderness. I even asked my Higher Power to hang out with me and to help me stop if I wasn't feeling okay.

I was being *sensual,* not just sexual. Eventually after a time, I brought myself to a stunning climax and afterward, snuggled in with a blanket and lingered in the afterglow with the candles and the music. *Unforgettable* was what that was. I had shown myself what sex could be like, devoid of shame, judgement, performance, escape, bondage, violation, manipulation, or the need for perfection.

When there is true intimacy during sex, compulsivity goes away and real satisfaction remains. There was no more hole to try to fill — I was made complete for that moment by my own doing, and I felt a contentment and a happiness the likes of which were brand new. Hooray for me! Hooray for (healthy, connected) sex!

After such a wonderful door-opening sexual experience, I now had an example from which to pave the way forward. I continued to get to know myself over the coming weeks, but it was less about "the *sex*" and more about observing and acting on internal drives, hormonal messages, playfulness, and connection.

Just like I had to learn that relocation/moving was never a solution for my problems and pain, so too did I need to learn to practice sex not to *change* the way I was feeling, but as a way to run *toward* a transformed and integrated me. I still was not ready for sex with someone else, but getting this part of myself back minus the shame and fracturing of trauma was a huge reward for all of the work I had put in on healing.

Some people recovering from trauma and accompanying sexual addiction behaviors can healthfully engage in solo sex, and others cannot. As with many behavioral addictions, the sexual trauma recovery path is especially unique and completely individual.

Sexuality is a part of every human being, just like our need for food. Sexuality is a broad element and every recovering person has to set her own boundaries around what sexual behavior feels healthy, authentic, expressive, and connected. It is paramount to have guidance from a team of people you trust. I always found that the best guidance came from people who had walked a similar traumatic path, and yet seemed to have what I wanted — I knew they were onto something and maybe could help me get to a similar place. I put in the work and trusted those people as well as the 12-step and therapeutic process and it paid off.

A few months went by uneventfully. My job was still a struggle sometimes, but I was learning new things every day. My meetings and therapy sessions were a weekly place for continued "tweaking" in my recovery process. I had begun to attend a weekly experiential therapy group to gain more practice living beyond the filter of trauma. My divorce was soon to be final. My debt was slowly, slowly dropping, and with the help of family and a couple of well-timed extra fitness gigs, I was even able to take Blaire on vacation out west to the mountains in early spring of 2008. And, I started to explore *real* dating.

I had to redefine what it meant to "date." I don't think I ever really did it right. Today my understanding of dating is that it is a way to get to know someone to whom you might be attracted. Dating provides a pathway to understand another person in a fun atmosphere designed to show both people where they might have similarities and differences, and how they each approach things like values, work ethic, spirituality or religion, personal finances, partnership, commitment in relationships, sexuality, among others.

If we are looking for a life partner or marriage, dating is a way to audition potential mates in what is hopefully an enjoyable and fulfilling process of discovery. Mistakes will be made and awful dates will probably happen just about as much as fantastic ones, but hopefully the dater gets closer over time to finding out how to attract and enjoy and learn within a close, loving, fun, and mutually respectful relationship, regardless of whether it ends in marriage.

My dating process up until this point in my recovery had been: Meet some (usually older) guy I thought was cute, immediately get suggestive and physical, get very serious and obsessive, and then either move in with him or get married, or on the flip side, wonder why he never called me again. Not a very functional dating approach, to say the least. I might as well have called it the *Trauma-Informed Dating Methodology.*

So now I was learning some different tools, first of which was to *allow* someone to invite me on a date. Timothy was a member at the gym where I worked. He was adorable, tall, and *younger* than me by a few years — a total switch from the type of man to whom I was normally attracted. He sought me out at the gym a few times for casual conversation. This felt very nice — there was nothing suggestive or tremendously flirty about our communication, it was all very straightforward and *friendly.* What a concept! After a couple of weeks, he asked if he could fix dinner for me. How normal!

We ended up having a great date — he cooked a delicious meal at my home, we ate it while enjoying pleasant and engaging conversation on a variety of topics, we watched a movie, we kissed each other for a little while on the couch, and he left. We went out on a few more dates like that before discovering our life paths just did not move in a parallel direction, and we parted as friends. Though I was a little sad we were not going to be more to each other, it was a human response to a small goodbye and it passed quickly and my life went on very nicely.

A little into the spring of 2008, I met a man named Mark while out dancing and then again in an Al-Anon meeting. He was an amazing dance partner and we connected right away with that mutual interest. He was a few years older than me but the age gap seemed reasonable. Mark was sweet and friendly and endearingly shy. He invited me out a few times for dancing and we had a great time together. We continued to go out with a fair bit of frequency and built our comfort level with each other. When we did finally exchange a few dates that ended in kissing, the chemistry was not there and our dating changed to friendship soon after.

I went on a couple of other casual dates with other people. It was all really good practice at having a date be just a date — not a promise, not a proposal, not sex, just two people doing something fun together for a few hours. Though I wasn't always completely sure if I was doing it right, I was allowing people to get to know me. The real me. Not the me that felt pressured to flirt, sexually *perform,* or pretend to be interested in everything my date liked instead of speaking about my own preferences and experiences. My job was not to please someone else on a date, it was to start showing who I was to another person in reasonable increments, and to hope they were doing the same with me. It felt good to be in such an experiment.

Events in my life later in the spring and into summer of 2008 began to turn, and in truth, were wearing me down a bit. My divorce was finalized, and right after that, Blaire's father imploded. He overdosed 2 or 3 times in the span of several weeks and I had heard from his sponsors that he had gone back to drinking as well. Before the news of the overdoses, I wasn't sending Blaire to see him very often because I didn't trust his sobriety anymore. I had to make sure first that my remaining friends in Jackson or James' sponsors were with him or nearby if I took her for a visit. I was feeling overloaded with parenting responsibilities and financially strapped as well because with James' worsening addiction, his child support payments stopped coming completely.

I don't recommend taking this kind of baggage into a dating situation without careful communication and fortification of dating boundaries. (such as, limits on sexual expression or amount of time spent together, clear communication of where the relationship stands.) In hindsight, I think it was this life "blip" that sent me sliding back into trauma soup. It was around this time that Tom floated back into my reality.

Trauma often wears sheep's clothing and buys a nice dinner

AFTER TAKING A FEW MONTHS' BREAK from Al-Anon meetings where I was likely to see Tom and risk taking steps backward in my sex/love recovery, I felt grounded enough to return to some of those meetings. I really enjoyed all the other people who attended as well as the meeting content and the scheduling convenience. Naturally, Tom was often present and we began talking again.

This guy still made my stomach flip-flop. He was still handsome, still athletic, still much older than me, still hooking all my triggers on some level. I was managing okay around him by focusing on the rest of my life, hanging out with my "tribe," and telling myself he was just a friend.

We ended up going on another motorcycle ride just as the summer of 2008 was beginning — I'm pretty sure I was the one who asked if he would take me out on the bike, and we made plans to spend the better part of a late May Monday cruising around the countryside. I was excited about the chance to go, but also mindful of my tendencies, and so put on a suit of armor of sorts before we set out in the morning.

I enjoyed myself immensely riding around behind him in the warm Tennessee sunshine, but in my head I maintained some emotional distance. I also knew that this was just a friendly outing and not something I wanted or expected to turn into a relationship.

At the end of the ride I was actually pretty psyched that I held up some good boundaries. We did not get physical with each other, other than some hugging or hand-holding throughout the afternoon. I was not expecting him to call me the next day or anytime soon, and I knew I would probably see him at an Al-Anon meeting here and there, per usual.

Another month went by and we saw each other as expected at meetings and talked on the phone a time or two. All appeared well with my insides and I continued to deal with my life — the good stuff of parenting, work, and being social, as well as the bad stuff with Blaire's father and his continuing struggles. So, I was surprised and delighted when Tom emailed me out of the blue to ask me out on a real date.

Still mindful about emotional distance and a bit of armor, I told him I wasn't available right away because of Blaire. We made plans for dinner and a movie several days out from the email invitation during a weeks-long stretch when Blaire was scheduled to visit the grandparents up north.

Having all this time between seeing Tom outside of meetings seemed a kind of courtship, and I was enjoying it. This process was unfolding in a very lovely way. Progress was slow and relaxed. I felt thrilled with myself for "playing it cool" around someone to whom I was so attracted. I was being invited into connection in a way that felt respectful and fun. I could not wait for our date!

In mid-July 2008, the fateful Saturday arrived. Even with the previous months of dating "practice," it had been a long while since I had been out for a romantic evening like this. I pulled out all the stops and dressed up, with high heels and earrings and makeup and perfume! (A rarity for me, being something of a gym rat by day and a mommy by night.)

I remember feeling feminine, special, attractive, and bubbly that evening. I enjoyed all the preparation almost as much as the look on Tom's face when he came to pick me up.

The attention from him shifted when he saw me that night — he looked at me differently — there was excitement and intrigue in his eyes. I know that for me my feelings of attraction for Tom had been simmering for over a year and now it seemed as though he was catching up to me in that department, or perhaps he had also been doing his own simmering. His attentive gaze was intoxicating and I wondered where we would lead each other at the end of the evening. I had the impression that the gloves were coming off for both of us and that there was a lot of sexual energy behind our mutual curiosity.

Even now I can see and feel myself laughing with him over dinner, leaning in, exchanging meaningful stares and familiar, intimate smiles. Our chemistry that evening was thick and enveloping like a strawberry glaze — delicious and sweet and sexy and satisfying — and we hadn't even finished with dinner!

After our meal we walked over to the movie theater. It seemed we were getting closer and closer together until we melted into a puddle of warmth and touch and attraction. We could not stop holding onto each other through the movie, and when it was over, I invited him back to my place.

We practically fell into bed together. It had been such a long, dry season for me between partners — two and a half *years* — *I* was feeling so amazing in Tom's arms and it was enticing to escape for a moment inside a bubble of connection, warmth, playfulness, and yes, *sex*.

We had *sex*, and it was *wonderful*. I forgot my armour, my safe emotional distance, and I dove in head-first into all the sensation and excitement. We talked, we touched, we learned how to please each other, and finally, we slept. The next morning, we lingered over brunch together and he finally left. For a moment, I felt like the cat who ate the canary. For a moment.

Sigh… maybe I should have waited or somehow found the strength to tell him goodnight without inviting him in. However, I cannot deny the magical feelings of those moments of tenderness and connection there at the beginning. Funny how a *shit-ton* of terrible relationships start in the very same way.

As a stand-alone event, that sexual experience felt good. There was history between us, we had gotten to know each other and shared discussion, feelings, and time together over a period of years. It seemed okay, even though I was sticking with my pattern of being sexual with a much older, charismatic, affluent man. Though the aftermath of sex with Tom proved disastrous, that first sexual experience with him is still a happy memory. I needed one, because the next year with him was a total mess.

Reading back over this last passage, anyone can clearly see all the hallmarks of my addictive behavior rising up — I notice I am back in my romance-novelist voice, just like with Bryan, using the words "escape," "bubble," "romantic," "intoxicating." I didn't see it at the time (who ever does?), but Tom possessed many of the same personality traits that hooked me into Bryan — intensity, direct eyes, commanding presence, experienced, worldly, wealthy. He was also active in 12-step recovery, very spiritual, and kind and supportive in several ways. There was enough "good" mixed in with all the warning signs that I was able to befriend denial once again and blithely continue down the yellow brick road into the poppy field.

Today, I can look at this experience through the recovery lens. Any of this might have been okay for me, ultimately, if a few variables had changed. For example, if we had waited to have sex until several more dates, or if we were closer in age, or if I was in a less emotional place with other factors in my life. It took me a short time to fall into the addictive pit with him and a long time to crawl out of it. Though I don't regret this date and the ensuing rollercoaster relationship because it was ultimately important in my trauma-healing path, I don't really recommend it either.

After the high

I MEAN, TOM AND I SPENT A *LOT* OF (TOO MUCH?) TIME TOGETHER at first. He called me every evening when he was out on the road working. When he was home he and I went out, stayed in, watched movies, ran together, hung out at his neighborhood pool, and we even picked fresh blackberries from the wild berry patch near the side of the road to have with breakfast the mornings he stayed over at my house.

There was just *so* much sex in there too. In post-coital delirium, we talked about moving to an island with Blaire or sailing around the world. Suggestions like this were pretty much all nails in my recovery coffin. He might as well have been mainlining love-heroin right into my veins, and all I wanted was *more*.

Anyone knows that the first few weeks in heavy infatuation with someone pass by in a blur of mushy phone calls, texts, emails, and snapchats, coupled with spending every available moment together creating excuses to be sexual and fantasize about forever.

Tom was really good at helping both of us do that. He traveled for work during the week, so that made our time together on the weekends that much more urgent and "special." He called me every night before going to sleep and we spent those first few weekends together moving as a pair between our houses. It was very easy to leave reality behind for a little while with Blaire still gone as well and safely enjoying her grandparents.

I didn't realize at the time that I was getting drawn deeper and deeper into my repeating trauma behavior because it all was such a whirlwind of intensity and euphoria. This man was pushing all my traumatic/addictive buttons early on and I was so high that my inner teenager was right back in the driver's seat. Plus, I was still keeping "current" sporadically with my sponsor from SA (but not going to SA meetings), still going to meetings in Al-Anon, and so I thought I was completely okay — a model of healthy dating and sex.

About SA (Sexaholics Anonymous) — I was beginning to feel extremely limited by that group. I appreciated the friendships and accountability it offered, but the group definition of sobriety (no sex with self, no sex outside of marriage, therefore no room for homosexuality at that time) felt really confining to me as well as being against my principle of accepting and embracing gay friends and family just as they are. I slowly stopped going to meetings after I had my self-sex discovery, but I held onto the friendships with my sponsor and a few other group members for another year or so until I found a sexual recovery group that felt more open while still providing a sobriety marker, as well as making room for gay sexuality — which felt more in keeping with my own values. Without a recovery group in which I felt comfortable and accepted, I was much more susceptible to repeating old patterns.

I was very quickly putting Tom up on the same pedestal I had built for Bryan so many years before — the pedestal of the perfect man — wealthy, wise, experienced, handsome, fit, competent, dashing. I was drawn in by the possibility of another savior — a knight in shining armor to take me away from the reality of single parenthood, financial struggles, and an ex-husband with a raging drug addiction. I kind of feel sorry for Tom about that. There was no way for him to be human and be with me, really. I had not healed enough yet to allow him that. And if I had, we probably never would have gotten involved in the first place. We do the best we can with the information we have a the time. In the words of Maya Angelou, "when we know better, we *do* better." So it was with me.

Tom and I went together to retrieve Blaire a couple of weeks later. He was going to visit his parents in Northern Indiana, about three hours from where I was headed to pick up my daughter from my relatives. We killed two birds with one stone.

There were all sorts of mistakes in this decision. It was too soon for me to meet his parents — their whole family relationship was fraught with unresolved trauma and abuse from Tom's childhood (big, sarcastic surprise with a large side of eye roll). I wasn't ready for that. It was too soon for Tom to meet my whole family too — we were picking up Blaire at my semi-annual family reunion containing several dozen of my nuclear and extended relations — *yikes*, to say the least. It was too soon to expose Blaire to the new status of Tom-and-I at that time. She knew him, but still she struggled with our new togetherness.

And yet, we pressed on together in the name of new love and fuel savings. The entire trip was trying. Staying with Tom's parents was weird and a bit uncomfortable. Introducing him to my family was awkward. Getting Blaire back was a hefty dose of reality and I wasn't sure if Tom was up for a front-row seat on parenthood, being as he made it through 51 years without one single urge to procreate.

We somehow made it back to Nashville in exhausted fashion, I got Blaire back home, and waited for Tom to not call. I was sure he was done with me.

I sort of had this thing with calling Tom. I thought (mistakenly) that if I waited for him to call me instead of picking up the phone first, then I was still in my recovery and not getting in too deep. *Hah*! Yeah, it was like a cocaine addict saying "I'll just do one line and never in the mornings. It'll be fine, really."

Lucky me, Tom called and continued to call. We figured out a "dating schedule," as it were, to include Blaire here and there in time we spent together, and I scheduled a sitter often so we could also enjoy regular intervals of time alone.

So pretty soon, I found out some things about Tom. Like the fact that he could not seem to make a clean break with anyone he had ever dated/had sex with in the past, except his two ex-wives. Or, that he never wanted to stay over at my house unless we had sex, because "what would be the point?" Those were elements of a person that should give *anyone* pause when engaging in a romantic/sexual relationship with said individual, I would think. I should have paid more attention early on, because several more weeks in, I was thinking we were in a serious relationship, and he made plans to see a concert with a recent old flame.

I had no idea what to do with that — I was broken in half with hurt and jealousy, but at the same time, wanted to "stay cool" and not be the possessive girlfriend. He went to his concert, and I went out dancing with Mark, because screw Tom and his stupid ex-girlfriend.

I had a great time on the dance floor, but more for spite than for me. I wish I would've chosen *me.* There are so many things I wish I would've done differently after finding out about Tom's entangled sexual history, but instead, my decision was to abandon myself and choose this man/drug instead. I stayed in, convinced I needed to change myself to be more appealing to him. Newsflash: that *never* works.

I wish I would have said something like "If you feel the need to see other women while sleeping with me, then I'm not the one for you — have a nice life." That would've been *so awesome.* I could not stand in that kind of power though, because already I was hooked again on the approval and the attention and the status of dating someone like Tom. 15-year-old-Leah was totally in charge.

I thought I might never "get" someone like him again, so I better just *make it work* which meant ignoring all my voices of better judgement and listening only to my shame-filled, trauma-riddled addict, telling me I needed to keep this guy around because I wasn't good enough to have the kind of relationship that was good for *me.* My trauma brain was back in the driver's seat and it would be too many months before I finally wrestled the steering wheel back.

Tom and I "cooled off" for a couple of weeks after that concert, and then after yet another Al-Anon meeting one day, we talked and made up, or rather I lied and said I didn't care who he saw as long as he was honest about it. The lie must have worked because we were inseparable once again after that. My pink infatuation cloud didn't last very long, unfortunately.

The relationship hit what felt like a nice pattern after a couple of months — spending lots of weekend time together with and without Blaire along, and plenty of phone calls, texts, and emails during the week while Tom was on the road. There was no more talk of going out with other women after that one time — maybe it was some kind of boundary test, I don't know.

I was just getting comfortable again, when one day in a playful moment I asked what I thought was a fairly innocent question about sexual fantasy — like, I wondered what some of his were. I was wondering what some of mine were as well, and was generally thinking out loud. I was expecting him to say something about lingerie or having sex outside, or something like that.

Instead, *Tom said he was curious about swinging with other couples and had tried it once or twice before in a previous relationship. He said he liked things that weren't so "vanilla".*

I'm just going to let that sit out there for a minute.

Because that's what I did when he first said it. Big, deafening silence engulfed the space. *Oh shit.*

I struggle to arrive at this part of the story. I am scared now that readers are taking in the last bit and thinking "what is the big deal?

Group sex fantasies are really common and totally sexy — how could she be feeling bad about that?"

The suggestion of an activity outside the norm of two people having sex was triggering for me on several levels. I was already sensitive to the fact that Tom had wanted to hang out with old girlfriends from time to time, which made me jealous and scared. And, after all of the work I had done to overcome the damage from Bryan's bondage and discipline demands, having to confront the possibility of sex that was more about intensity than intimacy threw me back into a traumatic response tornado of anxiety, fear, and grim resolve. I guessed that this was the price I had to pay to have all the things I thought were good about Tom, or anyone, for that matter.

With Bryan I could dissociate and numb out within the sexual intensity enough to push down his manipulative sexual narcissism and demands for a time. I didn't piece together right away that the same thing was starting to happen with Tom, but my body was telling a different story. I was preparing to go through the whole horrible experience of shoving myself off a sexual cliff, so to speak, so that I could keep Tom happy enough to remain the object of his approval, adoration, affirmation, affluence, and attention. The cycle repeats until we are finally able to break the chain.

Today's special: Trauma soup

S O AFTER TOM LAID THAT ADMISSION OUT THERE about enjoying and fantasizing about group sex, I started to shut down. I was at his house for that conversation, and immediately began to feel familiar knots in my stomach and shaking in my hands. I left quickly to pick up Blaire from the sitter, and spent the rest of the afternoon madly cleaning my house in order to not deal with all the emotions tightly contained within the shell of my skin.

Later that evening when Tom called, we talked about it briefly, but I can't remember what was said, exactly. I think he assured me that it was no big deal, but I got the impression that it *was* a big deal to him and would not be going away anytime soon. I was right.

A couple of weekends later, Tom began talking about finding a local nightclub that catered to swingers and being interested in checking it out sometime. I told him I wasn't ready, and that seemed to put the matter to rest for the time being. This was November of 2008, just a week or two before Thanksgiving.

Tom, Blaire, and I spent Thanksgiving weekend with his parents in Northern Indiana. Though I was super excited about spending the holiday together, (moving toward what I thought was a deeper level of commitment, getting closer to my holy grail of security/dependency with a man who met all my "check-list" items, no matter how screwed up he or the checklist was), our whole time away was a sobering glimpse into the messed-up, physically and emotionally abusive scene in which Tom grew up. At one point, his mother took him into the hallway, showed him a portion of the wall and said "Do you remember when your father pushed you through that wall?" I mean, pretty horrible and surreal.

Looking back, it is no wonder Tom behaved as he did in relationship with me, or that we found each other and came together like strong magnets. Trauma attracts trauma, after all. When we are not healed, we move toward the familiar, even when the familiar might as well be that weird and creepy uncle who wears too much cologne and winks suggestively at everyone while wearing a sinister grin.

For the record, I don't think Tom fully understood what he was asking of me with the group sex bomb. He, too had his share of issues to resolve and I believe his need or desire for "other" sexual intensity grew out of his own addictions (he had been an alcoholic) and unresolved trauma from his very abusive childhood. Even though I've processed through my share of anger at him and I fully realize that it is not okay to manipulate a partner into doing anything sexual he or she does not want to do, in the end the simple truth is that hurt people hurt people.

So, we all survived Thanksgiving, even if it came with an awkward, *I-need-several-showers-to-wash-off-the-crazy* kind of vibe. Blaire, Tom, and I arrived back in Nashville and began looking ahead to Christmas.

Tom and I had planned a ski trip to Colorado over the holidays. I cannot begin to explain how excited I was for this to happen! Skiing had been a major part of my life growing up, and the only skiing in Nashville existed in the water behind a boat. I had long dreamed of a partner who shared both my interest in skiing and my skill, as well as possessing the financial means to be able to travel to where skiing is. I had this in Tom. Yet another item on my growing checklist.

We both were looking forward to the getaway. Blaire's father had moved to Colorado (where there is all of the skiing!) earlier in the year to complete a real drug addiction and PTSD treatment program, and we were planning to drop her off with him and his family. Members of *my* extended family were also nearby in case Blaire needed them, plus I would only be a couple hours away if she needed me — I had all my bases covered — nothing was getting in the way of my winter mountain skiing fantasy!

More trauma soup, please,
and a side of hyper-sex

T OM AND I WERE HOT TO HAVE NEARLY TWO WEEKS of adult playtime on the slopes. I remember thinking "If I can just keep this relationship together till after the ski trip, I will be okay. I just want *that*." Like a dieter saying "I'll have fun this weekend and start eating healthy on *Monday*."

So there we were, shushing down the slopes of Copper Mountain on a gorgeous December Colorado morning — a blue-bird day, as some would call it, breathing in all the fresh air and high-fiving each other at the bottom of every black-diamond adventure. Then during one of our many chairlift rides to the top, Tom changed everything.

"I looked online for a couple of swinger lifestyle clubs to check out while we are here — it's perfect, no one knows us. Would you go?" — said Tom, nonchalantly.

Me: Silence. "I don't know." (*very* chalantly.)

Me: "Can I have 24 hours to think it over?" (trying to figure out how to force myself to like the idea.)

Tom: "Well, I just thought it would be a fun thing to try." (skiing off the chair)

Me: (at the bottom of the next hill, resigned and armored, the thrill of the whole trip verily deflated) "I guess we can go see it."

Ugh. I was pretty much resigned to the idea at this point that as long as I was pleasing *sexually* to Tom, he was happy (not that he did not care about me in other ways, but this was the way that seemed to please him the most.) So, I simply made that my project, put my chin down, and got to work.

That evening, after skiing, we drove into Denver to this place he had found online. I was so nervous I was ready to be sick, but we went up to the door anyway. I remember Tom asking a few questions of the hostess, and the place wasn't what he was hoping for, so we left. I didn't breathe until we were back in the car. This felt like a stay of execution. And yet, I *still* could not speak up and say things like "I'm not doing this." "If this is important to you, I'm done, I release you to find another person who wants this as much as you do."

Why was I so frozen? "No" seems like such an easy response today after all my healing and work. If I were presented with the same situation today, I would laugh out loud at Tom, turn to walk away, and find a lovely bar or restaurant for myself while calling a family member or a cab for a ride home. It drives me nuts if I ask "why" too much and I start falling into the self-flogging trap. The answer for me is "because Trauma."

Trauma response is so unique and so convoluted for each person who experiences it. I learned that my main traumatic response is often to freeze. I believe that the experience of being repeatedly bound and gagged by Bryan early on was a conditioning experience for me, so that when confronted with a similar trigger from Tom, I went limp, in a sense, and dissociated right away. I felt like it would not do me any good to speak up anyway, so my only option was to wait until it was over and try not to resist too much — have an orgasm and then I could move on. That was my coping strategy.

Later that evening and for the remainder of the trip, I reverted to being hyper-sexual with Tom. We had sex several times per day, to the point where he was asking for a break. Being hyper-sexual is a way to use sex as a weapon, almost. As if I was saying, "Alright then, if sex is what you want, I will beat you at your own game, so watch out. I will control all the sex so I don't have to feel what is really happening to me."

Here is my early sexualized conditioning from childhood showing up again in this behavior. Remember, the operating system still running in my head was "Be sexually pleasing to a man and then you will be able to write your own ticket. Sex is the only way to gain acceptance as a woman in relationship or otherwise, so get really good at it and do whatever someone else wants, no matter how much you may hate it or how damaging it may be. Also, don't talk about it and rock the boat, don't ask for what I need at all. Keep a man sexually satisfied at all times."

Life after skiing

D ESPITE THE ODD TURN OF EVENTS with the group sex detour, Tom and I had a lot of fun on the rest of the trip. To date, it was the best skiing I've ever done — and I was high and/or dissociated for much of the trip — a very odd juxtaposition.

I used lots of sex with Tom to not feel the hurt, sadness, and anxiety I had about his new sexual preferences, and all the rest of the time my adrenaline was on overload from skiing hard every day. These two extremes allowed me to live in non-reality for the duration of the trip, but once the intensity came to its scheduled end, I crashed *hard*.

The day after we got back from Colorado, my back gave out and I was physically almost immobile for several days from inflammation. The stress of "managing" my relationship and the traumatic sex it was presenting to me was starting to catch up to my system. I was less afraid of offending my body, though, and more afraid of not being able to be Tom's ideal girlfriend. Always a good little pleaser, I still chose being sexual with and for a man over my own true needs.

No escape: Frozen in sex

A FEW WEEKS AFTER THE TRIP, Tom did, in fact, find a local swinger lifestyle club in Nashville. He was very excited to go, and so despite the pain in my hip and back, and all the other symptoms, I went with him. We got all dressed up, as this was apparently a higher-class establishment as these places go, and headed out to see it.

At this point, my memory becomes a little blurry and I notice some different body sensations as I write. There are flashing images that come into focus and not a little bit of sadness and anxiety. Here is what I remember of that first visit:

We got to the club, which was located just outside downtown Nashville in what looked to be a bit of a seedy neighborhood. We walked to the entry door and Tom paid a hefty cover charge for us to get in. A hostess greeted us, asked if we were there for the first time, and said she would show us around.

As the young woman led us down a dark corridor, I kept repeating to myself, "You did this with Bryan and survived, so just strap on the persona who loves this. Be that person tonight. It's your job to be a sex pot and let go. You can totally *do* this — you're on now, so give 'em what they want." I shook my head, threw my shoulders back, started to strut, and literally became someone else in that moment — I locked my real self away in a box that night and did not let her out until months later. It was quite a performance.

The next things I remember are sounds and lights interspersed with images of sex going on all around us. There was a large dance area on the main floor where people were dancing in various stages of undress. I liked to dance, so this area felt a little safer for me. I kept gravitating back to the dance floor as the evening wore on. I could forget myself and pretend this was normal as long as I was dancing.

Upstairs there were couples and groups engaged in various sexual acts. Tom and I did not participate with any other people, but absorbed all that was going on and did our own thing once or twice.

There was one moment on the dance floor when I had a flashback of being chained and hanging from the ceiling beam in Bryan's basement. I told myself that I was "showing" Bryan a thing or two by going to this club and that I should press on through. What I was really doing was repeating my trauma at the behest of another traumatized person. I could *not* find my voice and I was *not* okay.

At the end of the evening, I felt a little shell-shocked. I remember Tom saying in the car on the way home that he thought we were the "hottest couple there," as if it were some kind of competition. Maybe it was to him.

When we got back to his place, I couldn't sleep. My stomach (always my stomach!) was churning and I didn't want to admit that I was now a person who goes to swinger lifestyle clubs. Since I couldn't sleep, I woke Tom up to have more sex. It was the only way I could numb out enough to finally drop off.

The next morning, Tom was pleased about the previous night and talked about how much fun he had. He kept making jokes about people in church on Sunday and how many of them might have been at the club the night before. I just felt jittery and wanted to leave.

The whole rest of the day I felt ashamed — I was a mother. I was trying to be a "good" girlfriend. I just wanted a normal relationship, and instead I had spiraled down into a rabbit hole of sexual shame all over again. I really believed that I had to completely sell myself out in order to be in a relationship with a man who would care about me and value me enough to invite me to do fun things or partake of his affluent lifestyle (never mind being able to create my *own* affluent lifestyle!) I began to feel a sense of doom that only grew larger as the weeks went by.

Even now, I question myself: Why couldn't I just say no *and leave? Rather than beat myself up around this question, I took it to my friend and colleague, Janet Yeats, a Licensed Therapist, who specializes in the treatment of trauma victims. Here is the short email exchange:*

> **Leah:** *Hi, Janet. I have a professional/technical question:*
>
> *I've been doing some reading on the long-term effects of child sexual abuse, especially on trauma bonding and revictimization. You know, where an abused woman*

will often return to the offender several times before breaking free, and/or how dysfunctional relationship patterns often appear in survivors like myself, for instance, picking out people with very similar problems/issues as the original abuser to get involved with. I'm getting a little bogged down in the language of some of these articles, and here is my question:

Why cannot trauma survivors seem to say no *to these revictimization scenarios? I mean, what is the piece of the trauma-brain response at work here preventing a person from seeing the forest for the trees when first confronted with a triggering person? How can trauma explain that some women (or men) literally* run *toward the people who are* worst *for them, and then are not able to voluntarily get out?*

Thanks for taking a minute if you have a response, I very much appreciate it.

Janet: *Good question, Leah. It's likely going to have a bunch of answers, depending on the situation and the person.*

In general, the reason people seem to be unable to say no is because of familiarity: humans are generally more comfortable with the familiar even if the familiar is uncomfortable. The familiar is known. They know how to act in the familiar. They know who they are in the familiar. They know who the other is in the familiar. Perpetrators undermine the people they are victimizing, usually in very subtle ways and convince them that no one else will understand them, will take care of them, will be known to them. The perpetrator may even show some vulnerability to let the person think that they need them. We all want to be needed, we want our life to be meaningful — maybe outside of the familiar, the person is afraid they won't be able to be meaningful.

A major second reason is safety. Which — of course — is completely ironic because they are not really safe with the perpetrator. Again, subtlety allows the perp to convince the person they are not safe outside of their relationship.

Hope this helps! Janet

—

Janet Yeats, LMFT LLC
Marriage and Family Therapist
AAMFT & MAMFT Board Approved Supervisor

Janet's response fits both Bryan's and Tom's behavior nearly exactly. While I don't categorize Tom as a rapist, merely very manipulative with a heavy dose of narcissism, the revictimization is clear. Tom was in a prime position to take advantage of my previous trauma to obtain the sexual response from me that he wanted, even though he was not aware of the scope of the effects of my previous trauma. And I, being a survivor, was inescapably inclined to let him.

So, now there was a new pattern established between Tom and I. Since I had agreed to go to this club one time, I felt doubly obligated to do it again, and we did, for several more visits.

I remember on one occasion being so dissociated while Tom was performing oral sex on me in this same club, I distinctly heard another person nearby saying "Look at her, is she dead or what?"

That statement triggered me to hurry up and have an orgasm so that it could be over and we could be closer to leaving.

I think we went to this particular club 3 or 4 times. Then, that became too tame for Tom — he wanted a place where people were more into switching and swapping, and so he began looking around again for a place where he could continue to push the "swinger" envelope.

Meanwhile, the weekends we did not visit the club were lower key — in amongst this secret life were visits from parents, work schedules, hanging out with Blaire, a Caribbean cruise financed by Tom, a "family" Easter weekend at the beach with Blaire, Tom, and myself. I was two people — a mother/professional and a sex toy. I felt split in two.

A funny thing happens when one lives in a traumatic/addiction response for long periods of time: the body starts rebelling against the trauma status quo. In my case, since my voice was *not* working to get myself into a normalized and healthy state, my body took over and began to make decisions for me.

At first, there was that chronic hip injury that erupted into a scary inflammation flare-up right after we returned from the ski trip. It took months to heal. I became so anxious that I couldn't eat, so I started losing weight at an alarming rate — to the point that at first people I knew said that I looked great, and then later said that I was losing too much and to please stop. I was depressed. My sleep suffered. I was grouchy most of the time with Blaire and resented her for intruding on my time with Tom, for which I felt immediately guilty.

I believe our bodies present us with pain and issues as one way to hopefully avoid more trauma. For example, consider a person who is tortured — if the pain is too great, the person passes out. No point in continuing the torture if the victim can't talk or respond. So, too it was with me — if my hip was hurting so much that I could barely walk, I was much less able to head out for frequent "dates" with Tom that would force me back into a traumatic sexual arena. If I was tired and depressed all the time, I could not go out either, or if my stomach was upset, I had another excuse to do something normal instead of something traumatizing. Today I am grateful for these big and small hurts — I think my body literally kept me from going so far with the sexual trauma that I couldn't go back.

Critical mass

THROUGHOUT LATE WINTER AND EARLY SPRING OF 2009, I continued to drop weight, have sleeping problems, and suffer with a riotous gut. I tried to balance single motherhood with being a sexual plaything. It was not working very well, and I would soon implode.

Tom was successful in finding a club that catered more to his partner-switching curiosity. I remember one of the few times we went to this new place, my parents were in town for a visit and were planning to watch Blaire while he and I went out on a "date". I told them we were going to a concert. Again, I prepared to slip into my alternate self and lock the real me away in her box. The whole day preceding the club outing, I walked around in an anxious trance, trying to get my skin to stop crawling. I was actually looking forward to the sex later, because I knew it would at least calm my symptoms for a minute.

After a surreal dinner with my parents at Tom's house, they took Blaire back to their hotel for the night and Tom and I prepared to leave for this new club. It was in a different section of town — even shadier than the first club we had visited. This place had a very different atmosphere — everything was older and seemed like it came from a bad 1970's porn flick.

Tom and I had a look around — there was a dance floor here too on the first level, and several "group rooms" upstairs. After getting the lay of the land and dancing to a few songs, we made our way upstairs to hang out near some pool tables, when another couple asked us to play a game of pool.

I so did not want to go down this road. I was just so sad, and still I was wearing the mask and playing the part. I didn't want to feel the sadness, so I walled it off by sinking deeper into my false persona. A woman asked me if it would be alright for her to kiss Tom. I said I wasn't comfortable with it, but I'm pretty sure she did it anyway when I wasn't looking — I saw them pull apart quickly and smile at each other when I turned back around.

I felt completely defeated, and *still* I had no voice. I had sex with Tom instead while we were there. A lot. The sexual intensity of all the visual stimulation and the group atmosphere carried me above all emotion and pain. We left that night without doing any switching of sexual partners, but I remember receiving a massage from several men at one point, and I felt powerless to stop the sexual snowball that was bearing down upon me.

I told a few of my close friends what was happening. By this time, I was attending only a couple of Al-Anon meetings — I had completely dropped my experiential therapy group, thinking I was so beyond all that and didn't need them anymore. In reality, I needed them more than ever, but I think I was afraid they would actually tell me the truth, or that I would feel compelled to tell *them* the whole, horrible, shame-filled truth. Both scenarios were equally terrifying.

The 3 friends I told about visiting the swinger clubs were interested/curious, factual/questioning, and alarmed/afraid, respectively. None of them judged me or ran away. They all continued to be my friends, thank *god*. I suppose they were a good mirror for me and truly were a lifeline during that time. I was close to making a crucial decision.

Tom and I went back to that same club a total of two or three times. (*As is true again of trauma, it messes with memories, and my recollection of our visits are blended together so I can't remember all the details of each visit, or whether we were there twice or three times.*) Many of the same things happened, but this time we met and chatted with a couple right before we left for that evening. The woman was missing several teeth and I cannot remember what the man looked like at all. It was at that moment I think I woke up from my trance and said to myself "*What the* hell *am I doing here!?*"

A desperate return to me

FINALLY, MY BODY JUST COULDN'T TAKE IT ANYMORE. I was drowning in most of my now-too-large clothing, my skin was a mess of acne and sores, I could not eat and I could not sleep. My three-times-per week yoga class was my only respite from the unsafe place that had become my life over a mere four months, and one cannot live on yoga alone.

I called up my doctor. He listened to my symptoms and immediately (do not pass go, do not collect $200) put me on a low dose of Lexapro, a common antidepressant/anti-anxiety medication. I'm thinking maybe it should just be in the water supply.

I was afraid to take the pills, but at the same time I was begging for some way out of the pain. Yoga was not enough. Sex was not enough and too much all at the same time. Friends were not enough. I had dropped most of my recovery because I was scared of the truth of this trauma I had convinced myself I was not experiencing, so that was not enough. I needed a decent shot at square one again, and Lexapro was my leg up.

A few words about Lexapro: Lexapro is the shit. Seriously, this stuff was amazing. I began taking it with shaking hands and headful of doubt, and within one week, all of sudden, my life had *options*. So many choices about who I was or what I wanted to do or how I wanted to be showed up as if from the now very clear, very blue sky.

What had been for the last 4 months a floaty, sticky, mash of flashy sexual images, sickly erotic sensation, physical pain, and hopeless resigned determination was now thrown into sharp relief against the pieces of life that were still healthy and okay (work, Blaire, friends, nature, alone time.) I could now pick apart the pieces that were decidedly *not okay,* and I began to find my voice!

I hope my readers are CHEERING for this girl right along with me right now. She came through a very dark and scary forest — she has a voice! Help her use it — scream the scream of liberation from trauma with me — AAAAAAAAHHHHHHHHHHHHHHHHH! Let's help her get all the way out — I've been waiting so long to see her triumph!!!!!

My first action in this new, clear world was to tell Tom I was no longer going to either of the swinger clubs. My second action was to make several appointments with a psychologist who specialized in Eye Movement Desensitization and Reprocessing (EMDR) — a new-ish trauma treatment modality I had heard about in some of my trauma camp groups. My third action was to take Blaire and I away for a weekend just the two of us — a thing I had been neglecting for far too long.

First, Tom seemed deflated and distant about my choice to stay away from the clubs, or maybe just bewildered, I don't know. Second, my new therapist began helping me dig deeper into my original trauma around Bryan and begin to understand the similarities between Bryan and Tom. She also helped me understand that it is really difficult to have true intimacy in a primary relationship when more than two people are involved. Third, the weekend away with Blaire created a safe place as well as some distance from what was going on — enough that I slept like a log, ate like a linebacker, laughed like a child with my daughter, and calmed the fuck down enough to start seeing the trauma-forest for the trees.

The choice to live a trauma-free life

W HEN I RETURNED FROM MY TRIP WITH BLAIRE, I felt newly empowered, un-foggy, and at least in "like" with myself once again. Blaire's grandparents had met us where we were vacationing to take her back home with them for her summer visit, so when I got back to Nashville, I truly had space to make decisions just for me. Breathing was easier, working was easier, sleeping was easier, exercising was easier, *life* was easier. I began to recognize myself once more — the *me* I had locked away in a box when I became someone else inside the swinger club started peeking out of that dark and empty place.

I had been sharing my process with Tom the last several weeks, from starting the Lexapro to the content of my therapist appointments, to how safe I felt in the hotel room while away with Blaire. He listened, for the most part, but seemed to be getting further and further away from me emotionally, and would quickly begin talking about himself or change the subject whenever there was a space.

In my trauma trance, his distance would have killed me. I would have doubled down on trying to figure out where I had gone wrong and how to fix it. Now, though, in this new and shored-up state, I could be in my own corner and reach for the unknown with optimism instead of terror. I. Was. Strong.

I got the feeling Tom was losing interest now that I wasn't accommodating his every (sexual) need or that I was presenting some challenges to the relationship he didn't really want to deal with. Maybe we were mirrors for each other — the fact that I was really looking at my trauma meant that he might have to deal with his own trauma on a deeper level and perhaps he didn't want to or thought he didn't need to. Whatever. It is all just projection on my part — I will never know where his head was during that time, just that he was pulling away.

When I got back to Nashville after hanging out solo with Blaire, I was excited to see Tom again. I missed him. There was this weird reality for me of knowing that he was in large part a very screwed up section of my life, but I still loved him deeply and I was hoping we could move forward together in some new way. I wanted to give it a shot, at any rate.

Tom and I reunited happily at his home, but more of his distance quickly surfaced. It was Memorial Day weekend, 2009 — we did normal things like cooking meals, shopping, jogging, and sex — although with the sex I was beginning to feel like a means to an end. Like I didn't even need to be there during sex because Tom was mainly concerned with getting off rather than getting close. The romance and machismo and intensity I had mistaken for caring and love early on were now clearly defined. They were also no longer enough — I was worthy of so much more. So was he, but he did not seem interested in talking about it.

I think that our intuition speaks to us in the simplest of ways sometimes, if we are really listening. Once I was finally able to listen, the truth of who Tom really was came through loud and clear in many tiny ways. That same weekend, we were walking through a crowded mall in search of a suitcase. As we marched toward the suitcase store, my foot began to hurt, and I slowed down. I watched with a funny comprehension as he soldiered on toward his destination, without noticing that I was no longer next to him. I thought "of course!" in my head as it dawned on me that he *never thought* of me as an equal, and I was in fact quickly becoming dead weight to him. He never had to say the words — his actions were a very effective megaphone.

As I was gathering the courage to tell Tom to shape up or ship out, I remembered something out about myself. One weekend earlier that spring, Tom and Blaire and I had a "normal" weekend together. We ate, we did yard work, Blaire rode her bike and played with her toys.

All of sudden I looked at the family mosaic we had created in that moment and I knew I wanted a true partner again — someone with whom to share a home, to set goals, to plan for the future, to grow old. I thought this person was Tom. There were moments like this when I was *sure* it would work out — that if we could act like a family every once-in-a-while, we could actually *be* one. It was time to speak up for what I wanted.

Goodbye, Tom, hello future

I JUST WANT TO BE DONE TELLING THIS PART OF THE STORY. It is a break-up, and breakups are never what we want them to be — we never say all the things we want to say and they never proceed the way we plan and there are always words still hanging in the air. There is running mascara and snotty, teary pillows, and the visceral sensation of a limb being cut away and a gaping hole where this person once was attached, like an outgrowth of ourselves. One of our selves dies when we split with another — the person we are when we are with our beloved — that person ceases to be. We grieve so much more than the loss of a beloved — we grieve the space, the loss of our uniquely reflected self in the eyes of that other. We fear the cliff-dive into the unknown, even though space must be created for healing to happen and for new blessings to find us.

I wasn't expecting Tom and I to break up when I had him over to my house the following weekend. I wrote down the things I wanted from him — from us. I dyed my hair for extra confidence and dressed up in a pretty outfit, thinking we might head out on a date after we had a chance to talk. Tom said he would come over on Friday but that he wanted alone time on Saturday and Sunday. Another bid for distance and control — I wonder if he still thought he held all the cards?

He arrived and after dinner I pulled out the list I had written down. I didn't want to lose my nerve or be argued out of what I was feeling or what I wanted. I sat down on the couch with him and read him the list.

My boundaries included a 2-person sexually *intimate* relationship, a plan to commit deeper with each other, for me to be included in planning significant future events like travel, and finally, intentional consideration of our respective financial positions — his being much more abundant than mine (while Tom did cover some travel and a few luxury outings, I was having trouble "keeping up" with him financially and could not afford to join him for all the trips he wanted to take or concerts he wanted to attend.) I was nervous but resigned to my requirements.

Tom was defensive and I think a little shocked at my decisiveness — these were lines in the sand for me, and this was the first time ever I had drawn them in front of Tom. Since I never really presented him with *any* boundaries, I can understand his bewilderment. I did not make this move as a manipulative tool or for a gold-digging gain. I had put a lot of thought into what was important to me in any relationship with an eye on interdependent partnership and deeper family bonds. Now that I was awake from my trauma trance, I was finally able to be a true *grown-up* in a primary relationship. Tom responded to this new me by saying how bad he felt that I had not gotten him a birthday present earlier that spring.

After several more awkward minutes of the break-up dance, I asked him to leave. I gave him a final hug and thanked him for what he could give — then he was gone.

I wrote that sentence and I can feel again the hole — the silence before the tears, because after all was said and done, I had turned myself inside out for this man and it was hard work and it came to nothing. Well, not nothing — there is learning in every deep or lengthy connection. The new space meant the sun setting, once and for all, on all my fairy-tale fantasies. No more believing in someone's potential. No more paying for adoration and attention with not-okay-with-me sex. Now there was only meeting myself on my terms, and thereby meeting everyone else on exactly the terms they presented to me — not what I wanted to be true. Any relationship from this point forward could only happen in truth, clarity, fact, reality. And the place to start yet again was with me.

Coming to my own rescue

S O I WAS PRETTY DEVASTATED THAT TOM AND I WERE DONE. Not talking to him all the time on the phone was hard. Not planning weekends together was hard. Feeling like I had failed yet again in a relationship was hard. Many things were also refreshingly *less* hard.

I slept easier. I figured out how to eat again and I began gaining weight healthfully. I found meetings again — ones that I knew Tom would not attend. I took *myself* out on some dates for dancing and local bands. I had more time for friends, quiet, reading recovery material. There were all of a sudden very large swaths of real estate in my brain that were no longer taken up with thoughts of Tom. My head was a cavernous and peaceful landscape for many moments during each day — my own voice was the only thing that echoed inside.

My old Al-Anon sponsor Deanna had moved to Nashville that spring and I got to hang out with her a bunch as well. She was very good at just *being* with me and not expecting anything. We could talk or not. I could have any emotion with her and not have to censor it. Crying was okay, sleeping was okay, doing lots of things or nothing was okay. I was so grateful for all these little anchors in my life that some healthy part of me had held onto while I was in the trauma desert. All the previous work I had done before Tom had meant a great deal, and as soon as he was out of the way, I could pick up essentially where I had left off.

In one of my EMDR sessions, I had a big breakthrough. My therapist had me go back to one of my most traumatic moments with Bryan so many years before — to the experience of being naked and chained to the beam in his basement. I saw that young Leah there and I could see how much she needed to be rescued and how none of the men she knew were doing it for her like she had fantasized so many times.

Immediately, I knew what I had to do. In my mind, I suited up in my sturdy armor and climbed on a big white horse and hoisted a rainbow banner up to fly in the wind. Then, I raced toward this vulnerable young woman hanging by her wrists from the ceiling, naked, afraid, and ashamed. I scooped her up onto my horse and covered her with a blanket. Together, we rode off into the sunset of my psyche, and she rests there with me still today — healing, breathing, gathering her strength. She is okay with me. Her mistakes and her trauma are okay with me — she is not defined by them. She doesn't need to have sex in order to be nurtured and affirmed by me. She is enough for me. She needs advice and experience from me without judgement. I finally figured out in that session that I am my own best rescuer — I no longer *needed* that in a man nor would I ever search for it again outside of myself.

With Blaire still visiting her grandparents for several more weeks, I continued to work through the aftermath of Tom. He had tried several times to reach out to talk on the phone, and in one vulnerable moment, I picked up. He asked questions, I said things I wanted to say. By the end of the conversation, we were discussing getting back together and going through some couples' counseling.

The following day, we spoke again, and he gabbed on as if nothing had happened — as if we had never split. That night, I didn't sleep or eat. In the morning, I wrote him a final email to sever all ties for good. I asked him not to contact me anymore. He respected my wish for a while.

It was during this time that I signed up for an intensive weekend of experiential therapy with some of my old group therapy members. I was there to hopefully exorcise the last of my most recent trauma garbage and to begin learning how to invite (a long time in the future, I assumed) a healthy man into my life.

The work I did that weekend revolved mainly around putting closure on Tom and I, developing stronger dating boundaries, and in general creating more peace and light within myself for what I thought would be many solo weeks and/or months ahead. The Universe always chuckles at our plans the moment we make them, it turns out.

How the hell do healthy relationships work, anyway?

I FEAR THIS NEXT SECTION *will be completely boring to the reader — normal can seem boring, especially to an addict/survivor who is learning to adjust to life between the extremes. For me, these next few months were a mountain of learning, failing, and trying again to get my real self to show up in relationship — to let her introduce herself a bit at a time to a man. The "all-or-nothing, black-or-white" boxes of trauma and addiction take a lot of work to expand. Even though I was now clear on what I didn't need in a partner, I really had to work on allowing my true self to be the person my partner wanted and needed, just as I was, without needing to be a sexual chameleon for love and approval.*

Ciaran (KIER-on) came floating into my life on a piece of white paper. His hard-to-pronounce name appeared on a personal training request sheet on my desk at work. Part of my job as the team manager was to match up these requests with trainers on my team according to the client's schedule availability, fitness goals, gender preference, and the trainer's area of expertise.

I called him that day to get a little more info from him and get him started on his sessions with the right trainer. When he picked up the phone, I tentatively spoke his name thinking I had probably butchered it, but he was impressed that I got it right on the first try.

Ciaran told me a bit about himself — he was a rugby referee trying to climb the ranks toward a significant advancement, and had to pass through some strenuous exercise testing coming up in the near future. One of his colleagues suggested he work with a trainer, hence the paper request.

As it turned out, Ciaran had specifically requested *me* for his trainer. He had been at the gym for awhile and had seen me training other clients. To hear him tell it, "I recognized [Leah] as very competent and more importantly from what I had observed, [she] appeared to actively engage with [her] clients throughout their sessions. I specifically requested Leah on my training request form; it proved to be the right decision." *I love this guy. Even his storytelling is so straightforward and square. He is a CPA — they like neat little boxes around most things. *wink**

So, he liked my professionalism when he saw me working with others, and he thought I would be the best trainer to get him where he wanted to go. Little did he know that most of my clients to that point were either past retirement age or new moms getting back in shape after having babies! Working with Ciaran was going to be different, that was for sure.

Training Ciaran was indeed interesting. The only men my age I knew were the few I worked with or supervised. I thought it was a great chance to practice relating, on a professional level, with a new frontier of men — those who stood a chance of being *normal* and appropriate for me to be around, for once! I was more than a little nervous preparing for our first session.

Ciaran's strength and agility training progressed well over the course of his training package, and he did indeed pass his fitness test. He was continuing to excel as a rugby referee near the end of our training appointments. He and I had developed a comfortable rapport, and we greeted each other amicably and chatted a bit in the gym even when not engaged in a training session.

Here's the thing: I *liked* him. I mean, it was different. I didn't get butterflies around him or feel flirty at all. I thought he was kind, straightforward, a little funny at times and willing to crack some jokes at his own expense. I enjoyed seeing him at the gym and looked forward to the several training sessions we had, but that was it. I felt friendly toward him and I wanted to maintain good boundaries. This was such a new concept — no intrigue, just two humans relating comfortably in a neutral setting.

As Ciaran's training package was coming to a close, I threw a thank-you barbeque for all of my clients and the training team, and invited him to come. I was a little bummed that he couldn't make it due to a rugby commitment, but the party proceeded as planned and I had a fun time anyway.

A couple weeks later, after our sessions had ended, Ciaran came to a yoga class I was teaching. And a couple more. I wondered what was up. After one class, he waited for me, and nervously apologized for not making my party. He offered to make it up to me by asking me out to a local watering hole, The Flying Saucer. (Totally great name for a bar, by the way.)

This is the part in the story where I become a spazzy, excited puppy. This puppy, incidentally, is the real me. I am so not good at hiding things like joy and excitement behind an aloof, impressive exterior. I have to give Ciaran props for sticking with me while I pretty much abandoned all ability to remain cool, detached, or sophisticated after his date invite.

"Sure!" I said, in response to his invitation. (I have always jumped at the chance just to be invited somewhere — sometimes those invites are few and far between in single-parenthood land.) "I just need enough notice to get a sitter for my daughter."

"You have a daughter." said Ciaran. If he was thrown off by that fact, he sure did not show it.

"Yes, you should come and meet her." (She was in the child watch area where I worked, and I was about to pick her up so we could go home.)

"Okay..." said Ciaran.

So here is how I now measure the mettle of any man: After meeting Blaire and having a little more conversation with me, Ciaran altered his date invitation. He did not rescind it after finding out I had a child. Instead, he offered to make our date a walk in the local park *with* Blaire along so I would not have to get a sitter. I was very touched by his inclusivity — here was the epitome of a man meeting me on every term I presented him as part of my real, true, self, which included motherhood. He met me there and was not afraid.

Sigh. How do I write about someone like Ciaran? How do I write about us after seven years and counting? Spoiler alert: We got married about a year after we met, largely because he was walking around without health insurance, and being a Canadian, he thought doctor visits were free. (He didn't really think that, but it sounds pretty good in the story, and he truly still doesn't really understand our messed-up health care system in this country.)

I have tried three different times to describe our first date, our successive dates, but each time, the voice is all wrong. I can only describe us in singular phrases and images that float one-to-the-next. Maybe my struggle comes from the fact that we are still together, still discovering, still being human right alongside each other, and agreeing each day to make the choice to keep hanging out and see what comes up next.

What came up next for *me* after that first family date were several things: panic, indecision, and frantic attempts to control things I couldn't. Ciaran and I were inseparable for about 2 weeks, and then I got very scared and told him I couldn't see him for 3 weeks after that. (I have no idea why 3 weeks was some kind of magical length of time when all would be okay.)

Looking back at some of my early Facebook messages to him, I can see my old patterns and sexual addiction behaviors popping up like Whack-a-Moles. Ciaran and I began to get a bit physical (no sex yet) right after our first date, and I think that was a big trauma trigger for me. I began writing sexually suggestive messages to him online and, when we were physical after our first few dates, I began slipping again into performance mode. I could see myself doing this after each encounter, and it freaked me out. Since I didn't know how to stop, exactly, I thought my only option was to run.

When I called Ciaran to tell him about my 3-week plan, he was completely mystified, to say the least. I could tell he had no idea how to respond to what I had put on the table, so he mumbled some things or maybe asked me a few quiet questions about what he had done, and then we hung up. I felt so terrible about the whole thing that I called him up later that day again to ask how he was and to hopefully not lose him completely. I am still not sure, a bunch of years later, what made him stick around like he did while I did my crazy dance. I remain forever grateful that he was able to stay present and calm while I figured out a lot of stuff with the help of my counselor and recovering peers.

I sprinted to my therapist and told her how sad I was that I couldn't see Ciaran because it was way too soon after my breakup with Tom, and that the Universe was cruel for bringing him into my life at precisely the wrong moment. She told me to breathe and take one day at a time. Each day and all of my feelings needed to stand on their own, and as long as I was communicating where I was emotionally with Ciaran, it was okay to move forward, S L O W L Y.

I stayed in my SLAA meetings. I still went to Al-Anon. I was back in my experiential therapy group, and specifically asked the group members for help and accountability to do *this* dating experience differently. "Right," they said. "No sex for 90 days." What?!

How was I *ever* to make that happen? I had no idea how to not have sex in the beginning of a relationship, because that is what I always went racing toward in the past. I also had to tell Ciaran about this "safety" boundary for me, and I was nervous to say the least.

Ciaran took the news well, though he was little pouty for a while. But, then some amazing things started to happen. The pressure was off for both of us. We had a *lot* of fun going on dates. After a few more weeks together, Ciaran did a totally sweet thing that I had never experienced: *He asked me to be his girlfriend.* This remains one of my favorite memories of our courtship, and I may have missed out had we gone straight to the sex. Just seeing his adult self asking such an endearing teenager question showed me *his* vulnerability and that totally melted me.

I think we nearly wore out our lips with all the kissing on the couch after dates. This layer of being physical was *so* amazing and I am grateful every day I got to enjoy just that much for quite a long time.

Ciaran also got to witness my trauma symptoms in action once. I had a bad flashback while we were out at a bar one night. Going in, I was fine, but then a glance at the band on stage with a flock of screaming women cheering on the floor sent me, randomly, into total panic mode. I couldn't breathe, I was sweating, and I felt instantly unsafe. Ciaran took all this in stride, collected our things, and ushered me out of the bar. All he wanted was to make sure I was okay. He took me to the car without question so I could breathe and calm down. Wow. Here again, by holding off on the sex, I could show myself that I was worthy of care and attention and compassion and interest, and I didn't have to trade sex to receive it.

I had the benefit of watching and learning about Ciaran too, in all his amazing humanness. I got to see his warts and his beauty and his joy and humor and his grouchyness and his triggers and his strengths and the chinks in his armor, and I got to decide they were all okay with me. I got to call him on the stuff that wasn't okay with me (and he for me as well!). All of it was just so lovely to me, even the parts of him that weren't so shiny.

All of the sharing, talking, and time we spent together slowly built up strong emotional trust. We made mistakes around each other — we stepped on toes and tripped emotional land mines. We worked through those things as they came up and didn't sit too long on hurt feelings. We were not perfect, but we kept stumbling forward together. I kept caring about him more, liking him when he was sad or grouchy or loving and open. He stuck around with me as well, even when most of my warts were showing.

This kind of relationship building might be second nature for most adults — I don't know because my relationship skills had all been trauma-based up to this point. For me this was a whole new relationship frontier. All of the learning was sticky, hard, uncomfortable, unbelievable, and joyful — sometimes all of it at once. Being so exposed and honest was often excruciating, but slowly I was creating my own sense of relationship *integrity*. No matter what ultimately happened between Ciaran and me, that integrity could now follow me anywhere — I owned it, imperfectly, for good. *Finally.*

And now, the sex

T HREE MONTHS! Woo-hoo, gloves off, now we can have *all* the sex! Except, though Ciaran and I were both counting down the days until sex was "allowed," when it was finally time, we were both nervous as hell. This kind of coming together was really different from every other sexual relationship for me. Instead of sex in the heat of passion, romance, and *escape,* this was sex as a decision — a Lego block in the tower of familiarity and of real intimacy that we already had under construction. There could only be *presence* in this encounter for us to work. We had done a fair bit of (amazing — let me just say how amazing it was) kissing on the couch, but that was about it.

Still, our first encounters with total physical intimacy were... Sweet. Awkward. *Hot.* Imperative. A little fumbly. Hesitant. Insistent. Deep. Quick. Lasting. Luxurious. Sex was all at once about all of the things, in addition to being really, really, *good.*

Sometimes there was big physical intensity and sometimes the whole thing was more snuggly. Sometimes it was hard for me to stay present and I floated off somewhere in my mind. Ciaran *noticed* this every time, and he paused, stopped, asked me if I was okay. Sometimes I was okay and just needed to be reminded to come back into the room. Other times, I needed to talk, or to hug, or just to stop altogether. Sometimes I would slip back into sexual performance mode, which made Ciaran recoil — I could see and feel him pulling away and protecting himself from that. So, we would stop, regroup, talk some more. I had never felt quite so *seen* in my life as I felt with this brilliantly imperfect human. I had never been allowed to witness someone else to this depth either. It's not like we knew every single detail about the other — the important part was that we paid *attention* to the stuff that mattered in the moment and trusted the rest would be fine.

We were, of course, as busy as teenagers for a while there. Then, after a few months, we seemed to settle into the sexual frequency of normal people over the age of 30. After the initial "newness" sexual frenzy began to even out, I struggled often with intrusive traumatic thoughts or memories and had to double-down on using tools to intentionally direct my thoughts to the present — to my body and to Ciaran. It was often difficult to respond to Ciaran when he initiated sex with me — I had to say no first before I could say yes, and sometimes there were a few days in between the no and the yes. Yet, this was somehow still okay. Not perfect and sometimes emotionally challenging, but okay. Nobody died. Ciaran still loved me and showed it. I stayed put and spoke up for myself. I asked him what he needed and wanted because I was *interested,* not because I was addicted to pleasing another for reward. The shadows we both dealt with were medium-sized demons at worst and fleeting puppets on a screen at best.

And the whole marriage thing, again

I IGNORED CIARAN THE FIRST TIME HE PROPOSED. It wasn't intentional, he just happened to ask during one of my space cadet moments — we all have them.

About six months into our relationship, Ciaran and I had been talking about a possible next step like moving in together. Looking back, it seems a little nuts how quickly our coming together deepened, but sometimes the Universe does not want us to fuck around.

We both had been through enough relationship yuck to know what we did *not* want or need. When it turned out that we seemed to fit well together because we had done so much of our own independent emotional *work,* a faster track *also* fit for us. I often shed angsty tears on my therapist's couch second-guessing the evolution of Ciaran and I and the timing, but she continued to help me stay grounded, to build trust with myself, the strength of my voice, my boundaries, and to reinforce those things by trusting carefully selected other recovering people to witness the process.

Also, neither Ciaran nor I were getting any younger, and we both wanted a true partnership — and maybe *more*. After denying the possibility for *himself* of having a family for many years, Ciaran finally started acknowledging his strong internal tug toward becoming a parent. I knew he would make a great dad, and I was willing to have another child — with *him*. He also was settling into interacting with Blaire, and was willing to work through the (sometimes really big) challenges of a blending a family.

After all of the mess that had gone before, I knew that before taking the "cohabitation" step, I needed to have some kind of intention out there about commitment. For me, that meant being engaged to be married. I was direct about it with Ciaran as we talked about our future. We had fun one week looking at rings, (no diamonds, please, something completely different), finding a design we both liked, and playing around with timelines.

Then, I let it go. Another boundary for me was wanting to be *chosen*. That meant that I had to wait for the other person to decide when the proposal may or may not come. It was an exercise in trust and surrender. Sitting in the space of waiting allowed me to reassure myself that I was still just fine regardless of whether a proposal came or not. I had been, so far, honest, imperfect, joyful, intentional, anxious, and amazed while attempting to do what had long been impossible — be in a purposeful relationship based on companionship, passion, shared life path, and *integrity*. Those were huge accomplishments, regardless of whether Ciaran and I spent another minute together.

It was a damp, chilly, really-kind-of-horrid March afternoon when Ciaran suggested the three of us head over to the park and the trails for a hike. I thought he was out of his mind. Off we went.

The three of us shivered and marched briskly through the misty woods, up and down big hills till we reached that back side of the park we had enjoyed on our first date. Ciaran asked Blaire to walk ahead a bit, and then he stopped and turned to me. For the life of me, I couldn't figure out why he didn't want to keep walking — it was cold!

He said something about how pretty it was outside, and other words I don't really remember — my attention was regrettably focused on everything *but* him — and he finished by saying he would like to spend the rest of his life with me. What?!

Once I realized what was happening and that this man was looking me in the face, asking if I would marry him, I started crying, said "yes," and just held onto him with an enormous sense of relief.

Though I truly was fine on my own, a sovereign person, a good and responsible parent (most of the time), a decent employee, and a healing, strong, and sometimes vibrant *woman,* I was completely filled up with joy that I got to share all of it with a man — a *partner* who was all of those things too.

The condensed timeline for Ciaran and I is that we moved in together shortly after his proposal, and got married six months later in October at the courthouse with zero fanfare. I mean, we went out for brunch afterward (at Noshville, in Midtown Nashville — highly recommended), but that was it. We did it right then so Ciaran could be on my health insurance policy, because he was walking around without any and I thought that was pretty silly.

Our fancy-dress-family-and-friends wedding was planned for springtime. However, we decided to stop preventing pregnancy because why not? We *were* married after all, and our teeth were getting longer by the day, so to speak. I also thought for sure it would take at *least* six months for me to get pregnant. Hah! Enter Ciaran's Irish Super Sperm. I was "up the pole" (Ciaran's favorite pregnancy euphemism, *not* mine) about two weeks after tying the knot.

My daughter picked out my springtime wedding dress — she must've known something I did not at the time, because she chose this billowy white sundress number that ended up being the perfect maternity dress, go figure. The following April, we married — again. It was beautiful — a sunny day in the park with just a couple of friends. We had a great party for family a month later, and Little Gethan made his appearance 10 months after Ciaran and I got married — the *first* time. A fiery redheaded Leo, he is a great kid and the light in my husband's eyes.

Speaking of Blaire, she took the engagement news pretty much in stride on the surface, but as with many blended families, she and Ciaran struggled to find their groove when we all began sharing a home. Blending a family is really, really hard sometimes. It is also really good sometimes. Everyone has to find their voice, their boundaries, their courtesy, and their distance when needed. The step-relationship between Ciaran and Blaire is never as smooth as I would like, however, they are both proud of each other and try hard to figure out how to get along together in their own ways. Blaire and Gethan are good siblings. He annoys her and she bosses him around, and they hug a lot in between. It's okay.

Our little family is still trucking along, 6 years later. We moved to Minnesota. We have had job changes and life changes. We have watched older family members pass on. Blaire is in high school and will be at least 32 years old by next year, I'm sure. Gethan is racing through boyhood at an alarming rate, like all little boys do. It is a quick wrap-up, this little greeting-card synopsis of the last six years, but the point is to get to the next section, which is:

Sexual trauma, sexual healing,
So (the fuck) what?!

H ERE IS SOME MORE TRUTH in the form of a quote from a new
student at my yoga studio: "Everyone experiences trauma.
It's just a matter of who is resilient and has coping skills." (We were
talking about what it is like to teach yoga to students in a residential
mental illness treatment center.)

Given the fact that someone experiences sexual trauma about every
two seconds in the United States, (remember, I mentioned that in
the introduction?), it is quite obvious that there are millions of
stories of trauma and healing out there. What is the big deal about
this particular story?

The only big deal is that I'm *telling* it. Many people don't. When
more of us tell the truth out loud about our sexual trauma stories,
more sexual trauma gets discussed, in general, so that it becomes a

thing. Exposure, discussion, and honesty are the *things* that can change policy, health care, law enforcement, the workplace, schools, churches, and every other place where men and women hang out together.

When women feel safer to tell their trauma stories, we heal in greater numbers and become a whole lot *less* willing to continue to allow the abuse. The more women (and men!) speak, the bigger the safe space gets. So, I am adding to the chorus of women who want our current rape culture to change. In the space this narrative creates, the safe space for disclosure for *everyone* just gets a little bit bigger. *Every* story, *every* truth is vital to that vision.

Also, there are gifts in every trauma.

Yes, let that sink in.

There. Are. Gifts. In. Every. Trauma.

Trauma: An unlikely Santa Claus

I T IS SO CLICHÉ to say that getting through bad stuff makes us better people. It seems that in reality, getting through bad stuff can often make us worse. Un-recovered trauma victims keep projecting their wounds on others in a myriad of different ways — generational physical, mental, emotional, and sexual abuse. Chemical and behavioral addiction. Codependency. Generational poverty. Suicide. Murder. All of the wounds we inflict on others are really just projections of our own festering injuries. So, on the surface, trauma claims more lives than it helps, let's be real.

However, when a survivor can crack open their "victimhood" for even just a nano-second and start asking real questions, a magical (not easy, not simple) evolution begins. Trauma is definitely about the shock and the hurt (physical and emotional) and the rage and abuser accountability (if possible) at the beginning. Of course it is. However, if we let it stay about all those things, we are doomed.

When we realize that our trauma-affected life is in shambles, when we stop trying to muscle through our pain or even ignore it completely, when we can stop trying to compartmentalize traumatic events, then life starts getting heart-breakingly, gut-wrenchingly *good* again.

This is the work of a lifetime. It is akin, I believe, to climbing up an emotional Mt. Everest. I can only imagine the sense of accomplishment that must happen at the summit of the world's highest peak. However, I know for *sure* how it feels to accept the rage, sadness, grief, and loss that goes hand in hand with sexual trauma. It sucks. But, because of that acceptance, I also know the relief of forgiveness, the contentment of gratitude, and the joy of love as a direct result of healing my trauma.

Forgiveness, contentment, gratitude, and love are on the other side of the tunnel of the fear, anger, hurt and loss of sexual trauma. What was the depth of my pain is now the height of my joy. Though hard-won, the life I now have was totally worth all the work. And it's *not* euphoric bliss — it is a normal, imperfect, love-filled, pain-in-the-ass, deal-with-everyday-victories-and-defeats life.

And here's the kicker — pain happens all time. It is the *suffering* that was always a choice. It took me 20 years to stop choosing suffering. Some people have a faster process and others move more slowly. I suppose it depends on what happened and for how long. All I know is that it takes what it takes to heal.

Once again, my colleague Janet Yeats says it beautifully, in reference to the stamina it takes to be a trauma therapist:

> "Trauma happens fast, in a split second. The work of trauma takes far longer to address. Trauma work has

to go very slow and make sure that all the seconds are attended to and processed. Healing from trauma can take a long time, the therapy process can take a long time. Sometimes it seems that work is taking too long, therapists can wonder if they are doing good work, if they are really helping their clients, or if they are unhelpful and perhaps making things worse. Therapists need to take their time and hold onto themselves in order to keep from getting anxious about the trajectory of the healing work with their client. It can be hard for therapists to hold a non-anxious presence with clients when they are not sure about "success" with their clients and are questioning their ability themselves. The important thing to remember is that *trauma work takes time.*"

So, the Santa Claus gifts that my sexual trauma process gave me were Forgiveness, Gratitude, Contentment, Love, and lastly, a soulful, embodied, intimate sexuality. From trauma. Let's break it down, yo.

Forgiveness

I AM NOT THE WORLD'S FOREMOST AUTHORITY ON FORGIVENESS. The people that deserve that award are the ones who have truly endured blistering amounts of sexual and other trauma, and who have turned their deep, dark wounds into stunning lives of normalcy and sometimes great influence and renown. I bow in humility to their experience, and hope that I can somehow manage to honor their journeys while sharing nuggets of help and encouragement from my own.

The thing about forgiveness is that it frees up space in our heads that would otherwise be taken up by maddening one-sided arguments with people who will never apologize to us the way we want them to.

Forgiveness is not about making sexual trauma okay. Sexual trauma is never okay. What is even more *not* okay is wasting precious brain space, creative space, productive action space on those people and events that have caused the wounds.

When we forgive, we release. We cease to perpetuate the damage that a person place or thing has caused.

Here is an example:

My ex-husband did a lot of not-okay things with regard to his parenting responsibility — namely, using drugs and alcohol, which caused him to lose jobs, which prohibited him from paying child support for several years of my daughter's life. And, he smoked a lot of cigarettes. For a very long time, I carried a massive amount of resentment around his drug addiction, his smoking habit and his motorcycle, because I viewed those expenses as choices he made that literally took food out of Blaire's mouth and shoes off her feet.

I spent many sessions in the therapist's office having it out with a picture of James I had drawn on a big sheet of paper propped up in a chair. I had to keep getting out the anger and then letting it go. I made lists of my blessings. I energetically released his behavior. I surrendered to the moment. I spent more time with friends. I kept paying off my debt. I kept sticking to my budget. I asked for financial help from people around me when I needed it (my therapist was one of those people, offering sessions for $10 when he found out what was going on with the child support — I owe a big debt of gratitude to that wonderful man).

It took a really long time, but as my own situation improved due to providence, synchronicity, and a ton of hard work, I found it was easier and easier to let go of those maddening imaginary arguments about money with James inside my own head.

Instead of getting better, he was sliding further into his spiral of depression and addiction. My anger began to be replaced by some kind of compassionate detachment. As I focused more on my own situation, my concern about what he was doing got less and less. I began to realize that what I perceived he was doing to me and to Blaire was in fact the result of his own unresolved trauma and addiction disease. *That did not make it okay for him not to pay his child support, but it did make it easier to release my emotional attachment that outcome.* It also became easier to take my own action through the state child support system to hold him accountable for what he owed to his daughter.

Another forgiveness process unfolded with my primary abuser, Bryan. Once I got some education about what rape actually was and that the reason for much of my destructive behavior during my first marriage was because Bryan raped me, I could stop blaming *myself* and start getting *angry* with *him*. The anger was of paramount importance in getting through to forgiveness. There are no shortcuts. I needed to get angry enough at Bryan to go back in time in my head to rescue the me that was his victim. Once I figuratively "saved" her, both "her" and I could move on without him taking up space between the me of the present and the me that was tangled up in his grasp for so many years.

Also, I know now that Bryan was/is a wounded person. I don't know what his wounds are and I don't care. It is enough to believe that if he were entirely whole himself, he wouldn't have violated me and my family like he did. *That knowledge does not excuse him in any way,* it just allows me to move on without his shadow popping up whenever I am vulnerable.

Learning all this also taught me that wounded people attract wounded people. I still have to be careful to recognize these people when they cross my path and to make cautious decisions about how much access, if any, I allow them to my life.

This does not mean I am not compassionate. To the contrary — many of the people I have worked with as clients and students have often survived sexual and other trauma. I love helping all kinds of people find safe connections with their own bodies.

Disclaimer: Everyone has wounds. Of course we do. And friends or family could be at the mercy of a traumatic event at any time. That doesn't mean I disown them or distance myself when they are struggling. What I mean is that I no longer have people close to me who are active in their addictions or so enmeshed in their trauma that they continue to hurt themselves and others.

Gratitude

G RATITUDE IS PRETTY MUCH THE ANSWER TO EVERYTHING. Gratitude paves the way to forgiveness and all the rest. And, when we are in the depths of despair, gratitude can be the most inaccessible thing ever. That is why it is important to start really, really, small.

That first ever Al-Anon meeting I attended, I was devastated to be in that room, but also completely grateful that I was not alone. Relief and gratitude are almost the same thing, I think.

In any kind of 12-step work, we are encouraged to write down gratitude lists every day. Some days (or weeks or months), the only items on the list might be "clean drinking water" or "indoor plumbing", but those items are still important and can move us a tiny step closer to a different way of thinking. When we think differently, we feel differently, and when we feel differently, life can become something again. Something of our choosing instead of something of our circumstance.

I still use the gratitude trick if I am feeling low, or triggered, or if I find myself floating out of my body and out of the present moment. A thought of gratitude (for that leaf, the sun, the warmth or the cool of the air, the strength in my legs or the dollar in my pocket) immediately puts me back into the "now." Sometimes I have to do it, like, 937 times to make it stick. It takes what it takes.

I know I am okay in *this* moment. Every moment I am *present* is one more moment I am okay — sometimes even exceptional! It is important to remember that we are still okay if we are sad or mad or scared instead of happy. Okay does not equate to being happy — it equates to being safe, at choice, present, not dead, and fully human. Okay means being able to reach out and ask for help or support, to tell the truth to yourself and others, to move wakefully through a fully human experience.

Every grateful thought moves us to a place of okay-ness. The more we practice gratitude (being thankful for any little thing), the easier it is to forgive those who've wounded us (they are still wounded, not recovering, still miserable enough to hurt others, still suffering consequences that perhaps we ourselves are not). We don't need to excuse our wounders. We can still hold our wounders accountable where possible. When we forgive, we let go of our victim title. We create space in our minds and our hearts for—

Love and contentment

L OVE AND CONTENTMENT ARE REALLY CONFUSING. While in the throes of my trauma, I believed that love was sex. And, that contentment was the attention of the person with whom I was having sex. It is no wonder that for many years I felt neither very loving, very loved, nor very content. Love and contentment *before* healing my trauma were all about external sources; trying to fill some kind of gaping canyon inside me. *After* the healing work, I at least began to understand that love begins within me, towards myself, and contentment is something I choose or don't choose in each moment of every day. The canyon must be filled from my own inner spring. Luckily, I have an amazing Higher Power (Source, Collective, God, The Universe, Goddess) who is right there helping me dig the well.

I *often* feel love now and I *often* feel contentment. Not always, not even close. I just have a good grasp on what they look and feel like, so I recognize when I am *not* in them, and I recognize that perfect moments of presence with love and contentment are both sweet and fleeting. Whole religions are built on somehow attaining the ability to *be* love and contentment, embodied, all of the time. I'm not even sure that Buddha or Jesus had it down cold, being they were still human and all.

If anything, the ascended spiritual masters show us that it is okay to be imperfect in our love and in our contentment. As long as we keep getting back on the love and contentment "horse" when we fall off, we are headed in the right direction. Here is the real mind-bender: sometimes my love and contentment look and feel an awful lot like hurt, anger, and sadness. Even in those moments — perhaps because of them — my contentment is palpable. The contentment comes from the *entire* human experience for me. I have come to like my tears as much as my laughter, because I know I will live right through all of it.

The more we practice our gratitude and our forgiveness, the more room we have within us for love and contentment. The more we practice making clear decisions about love and what truly makes us happy, the less likely we are to head down the destructive, miserable road with sexual trauma as our ruthless taskmaster.

For me, now, whenever I find myself far, far away from happiness or joy, I start asking questions. I question what is really going on, what I need in the moment, whether I want to keep the behavior /circumstance/relationship or not. Before, when I hit a bad emotional spot, I'd immediately start looking for answers in places where there are not any, like running toward triggering individuals, compulsive and disconnected sex, spending, or other types of escape.

Now, when I hit a pothole in life, I ask myself what I really need. Sometimes I am just hungry and an apple or a sandwich does the trick. Often times, I really need a nap. Other times, it's an acupuncture appointment, lunch with a good friend, the willing ear of my Ciaran, or a solid and sincere hug — usually from Ciaran as well, or one of my female tribe members. And then there are the times where I really need to go hit something. Thankfully, I own a small yoga studio where there are plenty of cushions and pillows ready to hold the container for anger and frustration until they are both spent and other emotions roll on in.

And, I have to ask for those things when I need them. I have to ask it of myself and others. I have to be vulnerable and risk that someone (sometimes it's me!) will say "no" to my request. I have to be okay with asking until someone says yes, or until I find a way to give what I need to myself. And, sometimes when I think I need something outside myself and it is not readily available, just the act of sitting still and breathing for awhile makes me realize I had what I needed inside me all along.

Sometimes, I have to recognize what I DON'T need, and be able to say "no" to it — the needy acquaintance, social media, TV, food that tastes good but will make my stomach hurt later, too much on my to-do list, one too many activities for my teenager. If I wished one thing for my readers after finishing this book, it would be that it would not take 20 years for us to finally get to a place of this kind of discernment about good self-care.

So, love and contentment are daily gifted moments that follow gratitude and forgiveness. If I go looking for them too hard, they find all kinds of crevices and shadows in which to hide. If I do my human thing, remember to breathe, remind myself to be thankful for what is working in my life, and to release that which is not, love and contentment sneak up on *me* when I find *myself* in a shadow or crevice. The most effective advice is always simple. Not easy, but *simple*. Maddening, no? And also just so beautiful sometimes that my heart skips and it hurts to swallow.

How to have great sex
after sexual trauma

T HE TRUTH IS, sexual trauma taught me how to have really
good sex. This is true because during all the traumatic
experience, what I was really learning was exactly how *not* to have
really great sex. And, remember, readers, we are talking about
intimacy here, not about intensity. Or at least, intensity as a *result*
of intimacy, not intensity on its own.

Back in the trauma soup, "great" sex was all about a certain
number of orgasms achieved when the man thought I should
achieve them, and all in a haze of sexual performance — turning
myself into the sexual partner (read: fantasy) I thought would get
me the most attention and affirmation and praise. It was a far cry
from vulnerability and actual love — two requirements of sexual
intimacy.

Now, I have sex when I have it. With my husband. My choice is to have sex and be sexual only with him. Monogamy and fidelity are both boundaries for him too, or else we would not be together. When we have time and energy and desire, we have sex. It is always good and often amazing.

I think that due to early conditioning in both traumatic and non-traumatic sexual experiences, I have a fairly easy physical pathway to orgasm. It is just how I am made. I know many people who have to work harder at learning to have/allow sexual pleasure. I also have an attentive partner who truly wants me to feel pleasure, just like I do for him. We are both intentional that each of us feel safe, have a good time, are heard, and are honored during sex.

Sometimes, sex is pretty regular for us, and other times, one of us is going through something and we have to wait for each other to be ready to come to the table. I mean, the marriage bed.

Not that I'm saying that wonderful, meaningful, intimate sex has to be confined to marriage. Nope. I'm just saying that I think intimate sex is most profound when you have other intimate stuff going on as well — like figuring out how to live around each other for several years. Going through a few hard things together. Being able to call each other on your respective shit and to feel safe in those difficult moments of honesty. From that place of solid bonding and vulnerability, at least in my experience, the sex can be off-the- charts-amazing.

Now that I feel completely trusting of my partner, that I have a voice with him and that I know how to connect with myself well enough while having both solo and partner sex, I find myself getting bolder. Braver. More adventurous. Experimental.

Experimenting with different kinds of sex after sexual trauma requires caution and care. We need to *own* our bodies and our sexual preferences. We need to spend time finding out what those true sexual preferences are. We need to know what brings us the most pleasure, joy, and connection as opposed to just intensity. We need to still be careful of our triggers. Here's what I mean:

I still have some brain pathways that create arousal in my body if I read erotic literature that brings in elements of bondage and discipline. I may be able to achieve orgasm and a pleasurable body sensation if I think about those images during sex with my husband. However, what also happens is that I am pulled out of the present moment with *him* when I use those images in sex, and then there is no intimacy. He could be there with me or not — my body probably would not know the difference.

For a long time, those bondage images were intrusive — meaning they would pop up in my head during sex without my control. I would be able to climax in my body, but afterward would feel terribly alone, guilty, and somehow damaged because my orgasms were tied to this ingrained train of thought that one of my rapists created during my trauma.

So, I had to be really deliberate about practicing new ways to think during sex. My husband and I will have sex, and during our time together, perhaps a disturbing/arousing image will flash across my mind. I have to notice what is happening and consciously redirect my thoughts. To do this, I might open my eyes if they are closed and focus instead on the image of my husband touching me, or I may open my eyes and watch myself touch him. Once I feel more present and fully in our moment together, I might try closing my eyes again.

Another tool I use is fantasy. *My* fantasies, not ones that were downloaded into my brain by someone else many years ago. I won't share the details here of what goes into those new stories — they are mine and mine alone. But, I do share them all with my husband, often while we are having sex.

What I think of or fantasize about, I tell Ciaran. Allowing him into my head during sex is another way to build connection, to show him how much I trust him, to encourage him to come with me in our shared story, and to have *fun* as I replace trauma-inspired thought with intimate and playful images. Now, more and more, those new stories are the ones that are arousing. The old ones, because they still play every now and then, are much easier to move to the spam folder of my brain. I then carry on with the very sexy business of loving my husband.

I would like to have more sex. Or rather, I want to *want* to have more sex. I envision sex twice per week as some kind of goal, like completing a marathon or something. I don't know if that will happen soon, simply because I have two kids who right now require a lot of attention. They both have activities after school, and though we try very hard to limit their "scheduled" time, when they are not busy, either I or my husband are managing our work schedules. There is just. so. much. driving.

So, Ciaran and I find ourselves having to be deliberate about scheduling naked time together. I am usually up early in the morning to meet clients at the studio, so my hard-stop bedtime is about 10pm. We have a precious window of time at 9pm to work with, plus weekends sometimes.

I desperately hope that as the kiddos get older that our windows for sex will expand. So, until then, Ciaran and I also have to create intimacy in other ways. I physically and mentally cannot go from the transactional relationship of our marriage (kids, bills, transport, schedules) to sex without some kind of transition. This requires intention of the part of both Ciaran and I.

I need for Ciaran to want me — to *talk* to me about his day, to put his hands on me in non-sexual ways, to ask me to spend time with him. When these things are present during the week, I can jump into bed with him fairly easily at the magic hour. If there has been a dry spell of this kind of activity, then I freeze up if he approaches me sexually and I need a lot more revving up before I am in the mood.

Also, sometimes with Ciaran, I have to ask him to move out of his work mode, or find out if anything is on his mind that is stressing him out, or that he feels resentful about. Also, he really likes foot rubs, so I offer them as often as I can mentally be in that space. (I *don't* offer all the time — it can't feel like an obligation, or that colors the experience for both of us.)

I have been surprised to find out that men (my husband in particular) are complex about their sexual responses. I had always assumed that most men are always sitting on "go" for sex. Maybe some men are. I think I have oversimplified this over the years. It is refreshing to find out that my husband is just as sexually complex as I am sometimes, and he does not even have a sexually traumatic past! Knowing he gets into places where sex is the last thing on his mind helps me be gentler on myself as I continue to heal and grow in my own sexuality.

If having a fulfilling sexual life is something missing in our present lives, it is so worth it to work with a qualified, trauma-experienced therapist. He or she can help us to define some objectives and work toward them while managing trauma triggers along the way.

It is paramount to remember that healthy and safe sex begins within us. When we have no idea what we want or need as sexual individuals, we can't educate our partners on how to treat us in bed either. Sex can become or remain scary and unsafe at worst, or uncomfortable and unsatisfying at best.

My growth continues today because I *talk* about sex with my husband, with a few select women I know and trust, and when needed, with therapists and other healers who can help me work through any residual trauma symptoms. Thankfully, not many of them remain.

I am also continually open to finding out new things about myself, sexually or otherwise, because I know I have this great net of support and love to fall into if I make a mistake or trip a trauma trigger. I have also practiced being exceedingly gentle with myself. As trauma survivors, we absolutely deserve our own self-care — I mean, haven't we all been through enough already?

Take back sex, take back our power

WHEN WE STAY STUCK IN TRAUMATIC PATTERNS or when we deny our sexual selves after sexual trauma, our violators maintain power over us, even if they are no longer physically in our lives. I think this is the most tragic after-effect of sexual trauma. If we allow it, our abusers can just keep taking this element of our humanity from us.

I have found so much power in taking back my sexual self. The reclaiming of this part of me has been much like sticking to an exercise routine or adopting new eating patterns — I have to make the choice to be sexually free every single day. I have to use my tools and go to my team on the regular.

Today, my biggest tool continues to be a practice of gratitude. For little things, for big things, for all of the things. When I can do this with a little consistency, my abusers seem so distant and so small to me. At the beginning of this journey I thought I would never be completely free of them.

And, here is the other thing. I have compassion for my wounders. I mean, much of the time. I wonder about them. I wonder what their lives are like now. I wonder how or if I affected them as much as they affected me. I hope they somehow found a way to heal their own wounds so they could stop hurting others.

My ego sometimes pictures them as shriveled, lonely old men whose lives came to nothing.

My higher self rejects those thoughts, ultimately. It took years of counseling, yoga, gratitude, 12-step work, and personal growth to reach this point, but I am free today. My wounders are no longer living rent-free in my head. And, the more I speak out about them, the more I hold them accountable for their actions. I am the triumphant one because today my life if full, I am content much of the time, and my sexuality is *all mine*. Trauma, at least with me, has lost the war.

Sometimes I feel more than a little embarrassed about some pieces of my story, still. It is really hard not to compare my story to other trauma/addiction narratives that are filled with marital violence, abject chronic poverty, child abuse or neglect, criminal prosecution, incarceration, and other more serious or permanent physical consequences of trauma and/or addiction.

My heart aches when I hear about the sexual and gender violence that accompanies war and destitution all over the world. I fully own that my trauma, while still being real and valid and damaging, occurred from a place of relative privilege because of the color of my skin, my level of education, and my socio-economic position, as well as the country in which I live.

While I have been told that attempting to mentally minimize my feelings and the effects of disturbing events is never a good idea, I am exponentially grateful today that I escaped even more profound trauma. Recovery of all trauma requires cultivating a large dose of intentional gratitude, no matter the specific type of suffering we may have had to endure.

I do my best to live in that gratitude as intentionally as possible and I have hope for all trauma recipients to do the same so we can begin to properly place our trauma where it belongs — in the past, as part of our story, not as a repeating thought-loop nightmare and not as a defining characteristic of our humanity. Let us all be triumphant winners by living the best lives we possibly can. Let those of us sitting comfortably in regions of peace and privilege be allies and supporters to those who cannot help themselves.

The more we all tell others that sexual violation of any kind is not okay, the more our culture can change. Tell your story. Tell your truth. Be the one who wins at this human, imperfect, sexy, scary, joyful, dirty, gritty, love-filled life.

Blessings be, dear Reader. Ah-ho.

Resources Section

H ERE ARE THE RESOURCES that were helpful to me in my healing and helpful in writing this book. Always remember that every healing process is unique and there is no one "magic pill" for trauma, though medication is sometimes an important piece of the healing mosaic. When looking for qualified mental health professionals, I encourage the reader to seek out those professionals who have previous experience and specific education in working with trauma survivors.

Experiential therapy resources

Onsite Treatment Center

residential center for trauma victims, professional development programs/certification/training

https://www.onsiteworkshops.com/

Phone:
Toll Free: 800-341-7432
Nashville Area: 615-789-6609

Fax:
615-789-5696

Address:
P.O. Box 250
1044 Old State Hwy 48
Cumberland Furnace, TN 37051

Experiential Healing Center

For trauma survivors and for professional training

https://www.ehcmemphis.com/home.html

Address:
1713 Lockett Place
Memphis, TN 38104
901-372-0710

Yoga

T RAUMA-INFORMED YOGA PRACTICE is becoming a thing in more and more studios and fitness centers. Check out your local studios to see if any trauma-informed classes are offered, and before going, ask the teacher what background and education they have, as well as finding out what the specific shape of the class is like in order to manage your triggers.

3 yoga poses to calm anxiety

Child's pose   Legs up the wall   Forward fold

3 yoga poses to energize from depression

Standing back bend   Bridge pose (only lift the   Sphinx pose
(place hands on small of   hips as far as your spine
the back if more support   is comfortable to lift)
is desired)

These common and generally safe yoga exercises, combined with slow and calming breathing, may help to manage the symptoms of anxiety and depression. These poses can be performed daily and can form the beginning of a yoga practice. Always listen to your body. Hold the poses for just a couple of breaths each at first, gradually increasing your stamina to about 5 slow breaths. Before beginning this or any other exercise program, be sure to consult your physician.

Book resources

H ERE ARE SOME BOOKS that were helpful to me in my healing and in writing this book:

- Here is a resource that explains the concept of hypersexuality, dissociation, and trauma bonding as an effect of sexual trauma. I (and I believe many others like me) could have written this paper. It explains a whole lot:
  https://www.ncjrs.gov/pdffiles1/Photocopy/153416NCJRS.pdf

- A wonderful book/author on how the body and brain "store" traumatic experiences is *The Body Keeps the Score*, by Bessel Van der Kolk.

- Patrick Carnes is another author whose body of work on sexual addiction was incredibly helpful to me as I educated myself about my trauma.

12-step recovery resources

T HESE ARE MINNESOTA AND NATIONAL WEBSITES, but the reader can web-search his/her in-state sites for meeting and event calendars within each group.

- Al-Anon: for friends and family of addicts/alcoholics, addresses codependency
  http://www.al-anon.org/al-anon-in-minnesota

- SLAA, Sex and Love Addicts Anonymous: for sex, love, romance addiction
  https://slaafws.org/meetings

- SAA, Sex Addicts Anonymous
  http://www.saatc.org/

- AA, Alcoholics Anonymous
  http://aaminneapolis.org/

- NA, Narcotics Anonymous
  http://www.naminnesota.org/

Psychotherapy resource

MY COLLEAGUE JANET YEATS is a LMFT who specializes in Trauma, Grief and Loss. She counsels private clients in her office and conducts professional development for therapists and therapy students in Minnesota and beyond.

Janet Yeats, LMFT LLC
Marriage and Family Therapist
AAMFT & MAMFT Board Approved Supervisor
4101A W. Broadway Avenue
Robbinsdale, MN 55422
janetyeats@gmail.com
www.janetyeats.net
651.336.6217 (phone)

About the author

Leah RS Braun is nearly always uncomfortable talking about herself, but is working hard on not dimming her light, because that kind of thing really doesn't serve anyone.

Leah's day job is: Yoga Studio Owner/Intuitive Personal Trainer, and her very cute studio is on the western edge of Minneapolis. Leah has worked in the fitness industry since 1993, and now spends her time trying to figure out ways to change that industry from the inside out. She provides professional development for yoga teachers and personal trainers on inclusivity, leadership, intuitive training/teaching methodology, and the general skills of the job.

She lives with her (amazing) husband, two kids, and two cats about a half-mile from the studio in a regular house. She dreams often of ways to make the regular more sparkly in many areas of life. Leah *really* likes talking to groups about fitness, trauma recovery, dancing, yoga, and lots of other stuff, so if you want to schedule an event, what are you waiting for?

Go to leahrsbraun.com to keep in touch. And remember, nobody will tell your story as well as you do, so buck up and own it. Blessings be. Ah-ho.

63920867R00184

Made in the USA
Lexington, KY
23 May 2017